FEARLESS
PUBLIC SPEAKING

How to Become A Confident and Eloquent Communicator

FEARLESS PUBLIC SPEAKING

How to Become A Confident and Eloquent Communicator

By Chris C Aniche

Disclaimer

Dedication

To the memory of my late father, Chief Christopher Aniche, the person who taught me "never to give up in life and the virtue of trying again." And also, to my late father-in-law, Professor Edwin Ngaha, who taught me to "keep calm because all will be well."

Foreword

Full and authentic expression – it's the goal we all seek. The value that society places on persuasive and well-judged public speaking seems to have increased, as we live more of our lives on social media, vlogs and zoom. New forms of interaction provide new challenges, while new social media stars raise the bar. If the stilted reading of notes ever worked in the past, it does so increasingly less now. Industry leaders, academics, social commentators – all want to talk in a way that changes thinking, garners credibility and raises curiosity.

The challenge to express ourselves not only eloquently and confidently but also authentically, sometimes seems insurmountable. Public speaking or debating is rarely taught – and can be taught badly, with some proponents seeming to suggest there is only a narrow range of styles that are acceptable. However, the styles that are effective are as varied as the human race, because the effectiveness of speaking depends on the appropriateness of the style for the speaker, the topic and occasion.

This is a revelation for many people starting a public speaking journey. I felt empowered when I realised that I could discard 'BBC English' and formal styles, to speak confidently as myself, to reflect my own style and approach. As someone who stammers and is from a modest background, I found power in creating a style comfortable for me. A thread running through this book is Chris Aniche's own story of how he found his own style and confidence, and the vulnerability he shares will resonate with many of us.

This book provides a fresh approach to public speaking – starting with the question of 'why'. It provokes readers to consider why they want to hone their public speaking skills. Beginning with your purpose in mind is crucial – and helps the speaker break out of a cycle of fear. The book deals precisely with stage fright – and how to move from stage fright to 'stage might'. This chapter reminds us that however worrying public speaking is, there is always a way to deal with it, to desensitise us and to engage with the audience.

The chapters on preparation do a great deal to make visible that invisible process of speech-crafting. For every well-known speaker, there is likely to be an army of speechwriters in the background, carefully crafting text. The preparation section helps readers write a speech well and practice it effectively.

Fearless Public Speaking deals with techniques for speech delivery and mastery of a formal speech that will help any speaker develop confidence and authenticity. It encourages the speaker with a variety of approaches to keep the audience engaged and reminds us it is the authenticity that counts.

If Chris' own story of mastery of public speaking is at the core of this book, his insights into fighting the fear, staying resilient and creating an approach that empowers are the take-away messages. I, for one, thank him for sharing his journey and his insights.

Finally, I will encourage anyone interested in mastering the art and craft of fearless public speaking, to read this book and follow the tried and trusted principles of confident public speaking distilled in this book.

Professor Deborah Johnston
School of Oriental and African Studies
University of London

Acknowledgments

I am grateful to many people for their input and support in bringing this book into reality. The fantastic support I've received from my beautiful wife and partner in progress, Ijeoma Stephanie Aniche, my daughters, Lysette and Christine Aniche has been phenomenal. I can't thank my beautiful family enough for their understanding whilst I was slaving away writing this book.

To you, my brother, Victor Aniche, I remain eternally grateful for all your love and support.

I am also indebted to those who have influenced my career significantly, people like Leslie Cuthbert, Bob Bowes, Adam Stott, Ross Temple & the Big Business Team, and my teachers at the National Institute of Trial Advocacy, USA.

To my pastors Anthony & Sally Ashaye, Lamide & Kumbi Soleye, Friday & Anthonia Odili. Thank you so much for your spiritual guidance and support over the years. I am truly grateful.

Special thanks go to Chidozie and Vivian Ononiwu, Patrick and Gladys Aniche, Chike Aniche, the Ngahas, Aunty Angela Lucas, Chief Wellington Okam and family, Aunty Tata, Noel Usuanlele, Harry Sardinas, Lily Patrascu, Donatus Okoro, Kenneth Igbinedion, Olivia Ola Joseph, Bob Obua, Kate Iroegbu, Dr Wilson Diriwari, Joy Edu, University of Benin LAWSA 1998 set and the members of the Oguta UK Association.

And to my living legends, my sweet and amazing mother, Victoria Aniche, for all your sacrifice and support. You've always believed in me when I did not believe in myself and saw the man when I was only a boy.

Finally, to my second mother, my amazing mother-in-law, Mabel Ngaha. Thank you for your love and support.

Reviews

Fearless Public Speaking, by Chris Aniche, is a positive, energetic instructional book on public speaking that will help you convert nervousness into faith in yourself and confidence in your developing abilities. Filled with specific ideas for practicing, it enthusiastically transmits excellent ideas for visualizing your performance, banishing your own fears, and enjoying the act of standing and speaking in public.

Marsha Hunter, CEO, Johnson and Hunter, Inc.
Award-winning author of The Articulate Advocate: Persuasive Skills for Lawyers in Trials, Appeals, Arbitrations, and Motions (2016) and The Articulate Attorney: Public Speaking for Corporate Lawyers (2010).

As a professional public speaker, I have researched and devoured so much material out there on public speaking to ensure I am always at the top of the game. Chris has created a masterpiece in his book *Fearless Public Speaking*. The book is a deep dive into how to overcome fear in easy practical steps. I would recommend it to anyone looking to gain more experience, overcome their fears, or grow their expertise in public speaking.

Adam Stott
Serial Entrepreneur, Business Coach
Founder of Big Business Events

Fearless Public Speaking is a well-written book on how best to conquer your fear of speaking in public.

Chris sets out in 7 chapters the Fearless Public Speaking System which will take you from the 'Why of Public Speaking' to 'Converting your Stage Fright to Stage Might'.

I strongly recommend this book to anyone interested in public speaking.

Efuru (Obua) NWAPA
Lawyer and Non-Executive Director
Inclusive Multi Academy Trust

This is an amazing book that will help anyone overcome the fear of public speaking. This fear is one of the most challenging and limiting beliefs a person can have. The system that Chris has developed in this book as a public speaking and leadership coach is one of the most effective blueprints to overcome the fear of speaking in public.

Harry Sardinas
Empowerment Coach, Author
Leadership Skills and Public Speaking Trainer
Founder of Speakers are Leaders

Fearless Public Speaking is a must-read not only for those who want to go into public speaking as a profession but also for anyone who wants to communicate effectively.

It is simple and easy to understand and highlights the crucial points in effective public speaking. I would recommend this and hope one day to see it as part of the curriculum in our formal education system.

Dr Ebele Uche
Senior Lecturer/ Honorary Consultant LASUCOM/LASUTH

Congratulations to Chris Aniche. He has conquered his fear of public speaking to become an excellent speaker. Now he's used his journey and experiences to provide tips, and techniques to help others follow his path. His book is rich with examples and advice for the novice speaker looking to become confident on stage. It is an excellent starting place for anyone who wants to speak to boost their business or career but doesn't like speaking in public.

Bob Ferguson-Speaker
Coach and Three times UK and Ireland Speech Champion

The fear of public speaking surpasses the fear of death. According to a report from The National Institute of Mental Health, the fear of public speaking or glossophobia affects 73% of the population. What does that tell you? It means that many out there are so fortunate to have a great book such as this, written by Christopher Aniche who is an award winning seasoned speaker to put together a masterpiece titled *Fearless Public Speaking* to help many not only to overcome your fears of public speaking but also to help you to stand out as a fantastic speaker that anyone would like to listen to.

In this book, Chris has simplified how you can easily overcome your fears and become a confident and eloquent speaker who connects with the audience and impacts their world positively. Being a motivational speaker, if you ask me, how important it is for you to overcome your fears of public speaking, it's of critical importance and if it's important, then this is one book I will recommend you read as it will help you to speak with confidence and poise and unveiling what you must avoid to overcome your fears in front of an audience.

Kate Iroegbu
Author, Life Coach
Strategic Consultant and Speaker.

"Phenomenal! Chris's book, *Fearless Public Speaking,* is an exciting book on how to overcome your fear of speaking in public and become a confident or an eloquent speaker. The book distils the process from a nervous wreck to poise and effective speaker who can speak with conviction and authenticity. It is a must-read for anyone serious about becoming an articulate and fearless speaker in any area of their endeavour."

Lily Patrascu
International Speaker
Author
Branding Expert and Co-Founder of Speakers Are Leaders

The ability to communicate is one of the greatest gifts God gave to humanity. Therefore, we must seek every opportunity to develop that capability as if our life depends on it – for it does. In his book, *Fearless Public Speaking*, Chris C. Aniche, offers the world a systematic process to conquer the fears and live your dreams. From helping you to understand the 'why' of public speaking to how to 'conclude like a champ.'

When I was a child, I was always getting in trouble for "talking too much," and today, I am flown around the world regularly to speak, making it my primary source of income, among others. I wish I had Chris' book to develop myself in the earlier days of my twenty-something year speaking career.

Whether you wish to be a professional, paid speaker or not, your success depends on 'Fearless Public Speaking.' So, get copies for yourself, family members, associates, congregations, employees, and everyone you love. The more you speak publicly, the more your confidence grows as well as your influence and eventually income.

Chris, thanks for sharing this wealth of knowledge in a book. I will cherish it as your contribution to humanity for generations to come. Indeed, may all your readers conclude like champs!!

Alex Ihama
President
International School of Greatness (ISG), Global Strategist
Executive Coach & Professional Speaker
Orchestrating the Ultimate Training Experience Globally

Fearless Public Speaking is a very readable book, full of action-able and practical ideas, contrary to some other books that just say, 'Act confident and look people in the eye!' It's written from personal experience and includes an excellent acronym to guide you through your public speaking steps. Overcome your fear of public speaking now! I highly recommend it.

Bob Bowes
Consultant
Communicator & Distinguished Toastmaster

"You gain strength, courage and confidence by every experience in which you really stop to look fear in the face. You are able to say to yourself, 'I have lived through this horror. I can take the next thing that comes along.' You must do the thing you think you cannot do."

— ELEANOR ROOSEVELT

Table of Contents

INTRODUCTION

"Students of public speaking continually ask, 'How can I overcome self-consciousness and the fear that paralyses me before an audience?' Did you ever notice in looking from a train window that some horses feed near the track and never even pause to look up at the thundering cars, while just ahead at the next railroad crossing a farmer's wife will be nervously trying to quiet her scared horse as the train goes by?

How would you cure a horse that is afraid of cars—graze him in a back-woods lot where he would never see steam-engines or automobiles, or drive or pasture him where he would frequently see the machines?

Apply horse-sense to ridding yourself of self-consciousness and fear: face an audience as frequently as you can, and you will soon stop being shy. You can never attain freedom from stage-fright by reading a treatise. A book may give you excellent suggestions on how best to conduct yourself in the water, but sooner or later you must get wet, perhaps even struggle and be 'half scared to death.' There are a great many 'wetless' bathing suits worn at the seashore, but no one ever learns to swim in them. To plunge is the only way."

— DALE BRECKENRIDGE CARNEGIE,
THE ART OF PUBLIC SPEAKING

Speaking in public requires not only the power of oratory but skill and a flair for message delivery. Standing in front of a crowd is one thing; delivering the message is another. People speak for a myriad of reasons, which range from informative, educative, persuasive, and entertainment purposes, and this can be done on and off stage. While there is no one way to deliver a message, an excellent public speaker must master his or her craft before standing in front of an audience. I used to be so afraid of speaking. When I was much younger, people made fun of me because of a speech impediment I had. It

"The human brain starts working the moment you are born and never stops... until you stand up to speak in public."

— SIR GEORGE JESSEL

took a lot of practice, self-awareness, and skill development to surmount those hurdles into the expert speaker I am today. As you may have read in my bio, the skill of public speaking took finessing in several institutions. It is the culmination of what I have learned that you will find in this book.

If you have been asked to speak in front of an audience, it is not too late to go over the simple steps again. The steps have been simplified for you. Without an understanding of these steps, you might freeze on stage or seem unprepared. If I knew what I now know in the early stages of my public speaking career, my mistakes would have lessened. But you are lucky! Experience may be the best teacher, but you don't have to learn from your mistakes. You can learn from mine. That is why I wrote this book – to help all those who have decided to venture into the art of fearless public speaking. At some point, we've all experienced fear, failure, and fatigue. You are not alone. I hope this book will help you overcome your fears.

We must learn how to speak fearlessly through assertive communication. Communicating effectively is vital. As a fearless public speaker, getting people to understand your message is a necessity. Your communication style shouldn't be aggressive, and it should not be passive. Your message should be direct, clear, and spoken without fear or favour.

"If you can't communicate and talk to other people and get across your ideas, you're giving up your potential."

— WARREN BUFFET

If you want to be a master in the game, perfecting your communication techniques is something you need to develop consciously. Over the years, I have seen people with public speaking problems who are at a loss on what to do about it and how they can improve. This book was created to eradicate that problem. It contains tips I have used repeatedly to improve my public speaking skills. If I can do it, you can, too.

Why do so many people struggle to communicate effectively? The answer to this question lies in the fact that our ability to communicate and present ideas are an invaluable skill that can make a lot of difference in our lives and careers. No one is an island, and for us to fully enjoy living, we must speak with and to other people. Even in your workplace, upward promotion is possible when you exhibit excellent communication skills. Top executives in the world will always intentionally move an employee, who communicates effectively, up the corporate ladder. We live in an internet-enabled world. This may be an obstacle to communicating effectively, but this shouldn't be an excuse. The foundation of public speaking is communication, and this cannot be over-emphasized. A fearless public speaker expresses himself in clear and direct terms without being disrespectful. In today's world, where there are a lot of voices speaking at the same time, it is easy to drown in the noise. Powerful communication involves passing your message while listening to others.

"According to most studies, people's number one fear is public speaking. Number two is death. Death is number two. Does that sound right? This means to the average person, if you go to a funeral, you're better off in the casket than doing the eulogy."

— JERRY SEINFIELD

"Fear of public speaking can be overcome with effective public speaking tips, skills and strategies."

— ROBERT MOMENT

As fearless public speakers, we must communicate our message within the time frame given with confidence and poise. It must be made clear that the art of public speaking is not left for the stage alone. Provided you have an audience, that's a public speaking opportunity right there!

If you can commit to learning how to speak fearlessly, you will overcome the challenges and connect with the audience. Sincerity and authenticity, while speaking to an audience, are fundamental concepts, but you cannot be authentic if you fear communicating with the audience.

"All those iconic presenters of today were a shy little kid back then."

— AAYUSH JAIN

Many great speakers you listen to today were not born with a "public speaking gene," as they also experienced similar challenges. As a child, I suffered from a severe fear of public speaking because my teachers always told me I wasn't good enough. Does this story sound like yours? While growing up, I was laughed at because I had a speech impediment, which was always a source of humour for my friends and family. I had difficulty pronouncing the letter "R," and as I progressed in life, moving to the United Kingdom and later requalifying as a UK solicitor, my fears remained. The fear of public speaking was like a shadow that followed me everywhere I went, and I felt unfulfilled as a lawyer.

My story of success drawn from a boatload of failures with public speaking was the inspiration for this book, and I hope it will also inspire you to get over the challenges you face. The objective of this book is to empower you with strategies on how to speak fearlessly and overcome your fear of public speaking. The chapters and sections below will inspire you to take steps towards fighting off the fear of public speaking as you rebuild your confidence levels. Remember that we are on this journey together, and you are not alone. Set your worries aside and embrace the possibility of being an excellent public speaker.

Stages of Public Speaking

Before becoming a seasoned public speaker, there are different stages people go through before they can become a confident and an eloquent speaker. If you are new to the public speaking scene, I created the Fearless Public Speaking System to help you define your fears and go through the steps in full confidence.

"If you're not comfortable with public speaking - and nobody starts out comfortable; you have to learn how to be comfortable - practice. I cannot overstate the importance of practicing. Get some close friends or family members to help evaluate you, or somebody at work that you trust."

— HILLARY CLINTON

FEARLESS PUBLIC SPEAKING SYSTEM

Stage 1: Why

Stage 2: Fright

Stage 3: Might

Stage 4: Prepare

Stage 5: Plan

Stage 6: Poise

Stage 7: Conclude

"It's all right to have butterflies in your stomach. Just get them to fly in formation."

– ROB GILBERT

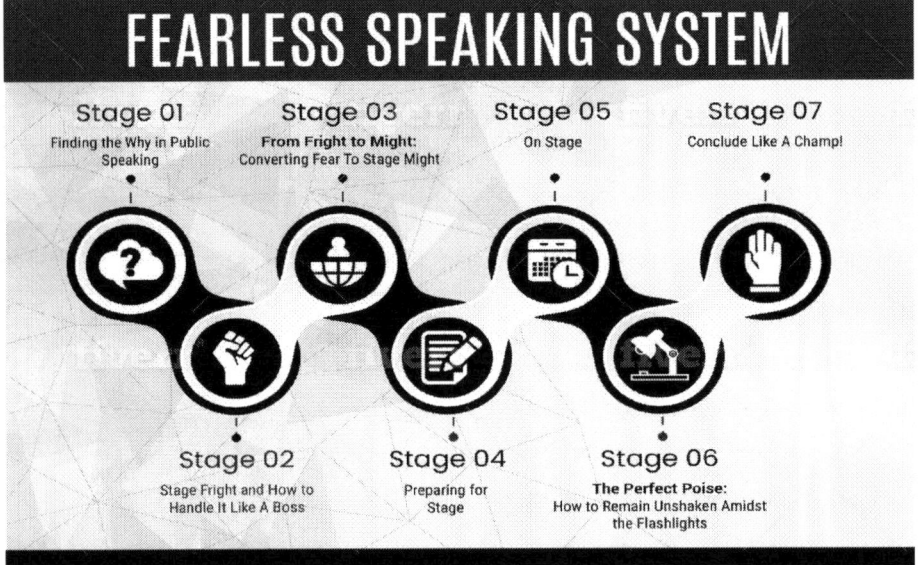

I will go over these stages in the chapters and take you from 'why public speaking' to giving a robust conclusion anytime you have an audience. Remember that public speaking doesn't begin and end on stage. If you have an audience, it is more than enough to hone your public speaking skills and deliver your best.

CHAPTER ONE

Finding the Why in Public Speaking

Chapter Outline

Nothing is as strong as a person who knows and understands the reason, they carry on in a particular endeavour. You hear so much talk about purpose and have probably read about people who have sacrificed everything for a cause to the detriment of everything else. Detriment sounds like a strong word to use in this context, but it is the one word I resonate with when it comes to purpose and the almighty *why*.

As an example, let us take Elon Musk and the work he has been putting into developing technology. Looking at someone like that go all out for what they believe in will make you ask what drives him. It can't be money because he has enough of it to retire and not stress himself any longer. So, what exactly, are the motivation behind Elon's drive and the many men and women like him? He must have had a big Why, a reason that kept him going.

Chapter Exercise

What's your "why"? Why should I read a book on public speaking? Why should I learn how to speak to an audience? Why venture into public speaking at all? Are there peculiar benefits for me to be an orator? You need to discover your why before going any further.

"We live in an era where the best way to make a dent on the world may no longer be to write a letter to the editor or publish a book. It may be simply to stand up and say something . . . because both the words and the passion with which they are delivered can now spread across the world at warp speed."

— CHRIS J. ANDERSON

"*If I went back to college again, I'd concentrate on two areas: learning to write and to speak before an audience. Nothing in life is more important than the ability to communicate effectively.*"

– GERALD R. FORD

Answer the above questions as truthfully as possible in the space below:

- ....

- ....

- ....

- ....

- ....

- ....

Generally, we must master the art of public speaking because communication is crucial for human existence. Regardless of your reason, learning how to speak in public is important. If speaking

"Communication works for those who work at it."

– JOHN POWELL

with people is inevitable, it means that lessons on communication are vital. But you shouldn't solely settle for the general idea; there are other reasons you must become excellent at effective public speaking as well. The answers you stated above should serve as a compass to guide you through this chapter.

4 'Whys' of Public Speaking

If you are still at a loss as to why you need to be a master of oratory, here are some 'why's.'

1. Speaking improves self-confidence

"Your ability to communicate with others will account for fully 85% of your success in your business and your life."

— BRIAN TRACY

People struggle with public speaking because they lack confidence, but something done consistently over time brings about improvement. When you learn how to speak fearlessly, you will become bold and be ready to take on the world. The more you speak and share your thoughts, the higher your confidence level. You would be amazed at the rate at which you can command people's attention and keep them focused while speaking.

"If all my possessions were taken from me with one exception, I would choose to keep the power of speech, for by it, I would regain all the rest."

— DANIEL WEBSTER

2. Speaking brings brand visibility

A brand is your identity. It is that silent, yet loud, attribute the public recognises. A brand is your trademark, your persona, your public face, or the being the public interacts with. Corporations, business owners, entrepreneurs, professionals, artists, coaches, and solopreneurs have brand obsession as a shared trait. They all understand the importance of maintaining a good image, and you hear them talk about protecting the brand.

What comes to mind when I say Gucci? What about Mercedes? What do you think about when I say FACEBOOK?

Can you see what I mean? All these organisations have an image they have sold to you. This image has been sown in your mind and will continue to grow unabated. Social media has made building a brand and maintaining visibility easier than it ever was. Now, with the click of a button, an outfit on the other side of the world can showcase and sell itself to an audience in a different continent. Social media has also made communication easy by breaking the barrier brought on by distance. Building a brand has never been this tricky yet easy.

As a public speaker, your brand is how the public perceives you. It is seen in how you dress, speak, and policies you are interested in. You are a living entity that breathes and lives the philosophies you preach; therefore, so much is expected of you.

Speaking publicly puts your brand out there. You've got to keep your brand visible! For you to have a recognisable brand, you must harness the power of public speaking and make your lucid thoughts known when the occasion arises. Public speaking helps you project the value of your brand to the world. Take Tony Robbins, for example. He has built his brand over the years by being visible. This was made possible via public speaking. Tony Robbins intentionally puts himself out there through consistent public speaking opportunities that have given a significant boost to his brand image. You will not struggle with visibility if you are great at public speaking because it is an opportunity for people to become even more familiar with your brand long-term.

3. Speaking helps you move up the ladder

If you are in the corporate world or business environment, you will agree that the goal is to move up the ladder. No one wants to start on the corporate journey and remain where they were at the beginning. The dilemma is, "How do I move up?" Well, the criteria may vary based on your peculiar industry, but there is a general factor that cuts across all sectors. This factor is the ability to speak and share ideas effectively; if you've got this skill, moving up the ladder wouldn't be problematic for you.

"Engaging in lifelong learning to improve your public speaking skills is far from drudgery. It can lead to a better job, higher profits, more donations, and public policy objectives. That sounds like fun to me."

— ED BARKS

Often, we think that those at the top only consider what we do within the confines of our jobs. But when a promotion is on the table, they also look beyond that and focus more on our relatable skills. What is the point in being considered for a senior position when you cannot express yourself to subordinates and those you will lead? Speaking publicly exceeds what is done on stage. Those who can expressly communicate will most likely be picked to move up the ladder, and if you want that, then you must be enthusiastic about speaking fearlessly.

Think about great leaders we all admire, such as Barack Obama, Anthony Robbins, Les Brown, and Abraham Lincoln. These are leaders with very humble beginnings who eventually became prominent global icons because they could address any audience and share their thoughts convincingly.

4. Public speaking is the highest paying profession

Public speaking is one of the easiest ways to make money. I once conversed with a renowned public speaker, and I was amazed at his speaking fees. He had made around £250,000 for a 90-minute speech in the London O2 Arena at the time of this conversation! Making six figures in one fell swoop wasn't something familiar to me. It scared me more than it surprised me because, before our conversation, I hadn't thought about how much money public speakers made. So, what did I do? I researched public speakers and the income they earned. I discovered top speakers, like Les Brown, Barrack Obama, Tony Robbins, and the rest got paid enormous sums of money for giving speeches that sometimes didn't cross 90 minutes!

Yes, this is very true!

It has also surprised me to find out that business leaders with the penchant for public speaking made money after speaking engagements because they could pitch their products and services while doing a great job of communicating their thoughts on a subject.

You can also become great at public speaking and make a lot of money while doing it like the people I have referred to above.

There is always a high demand for public speakers all over the world because there is so much information to pass across. Only good speakers can do that. Great speakers are needed in every sector globally, from finance to relationships, policymaking, business, and more. These industries will pay a reasonable sum of money to a person who can pass information to an audience in an articulate manner.

"You can speak well if your tongue can deliver the message of your heart."

– JOHN FORD

When you begin, you may not rise to the top as a speaker because you are relatively new to the sector. But later, you will surely gain prominence, and the more people listen to you, the more they want to hear from you. Great speakers are like a bridge that connects ideas to others, but few people can pass on this information effectively. If you utilise the information shared in this book and stick to the recommendations, you will be on your way to improving your finances through public speaking.

As we look ahead into the next century, leaders will be those who empower others."

— BILL GATES

CHAPTER TWO

Stage Fright and How to Handle It Like A Boss

Chapter Outline

> "The best way to conquer stage fright is to know what you are talking about."
>
> — MICHAEL MESCON

The second stage in our Fearless Public Speaking System is Fright. Stage fright can be surmounted. William James once said that "You don't run away because you are afraid, you are afraid because you run away from your fear."

This statement by James is true, especially within the context of speaking to an audience.

Some people run away from speaking in public because they have a lot of fear lodged deep within them. Now when you run away, you miss a unique chance to fight off the impact of stage fright. Letting stage fright build means you will miss out on an opportunity to develop yourself. Being afraid is not the problem. Staying afraid is.

OUR FEARS

"If you live with fear and consider yourself as something special then automatically, emotionally, you are distanced from others. You then create the basis for feelings of alienation from others and loneliness. So, I never consider, even when giving a talk to a large crowd, that I am something special, I am 'His Holiness the Dalai Lama' . . . I always emphasize that when I meet people, we are all the same human beings. A thousand people -- same human being. Ten thousand or a hundred thousand -- same human being -- mentally, emotionally, and physically. Then, you see, no barrier. Then my mind remains completely calm and relaxed. If too much emphasis on myself, and I start to think I'm something special, then more anxiety, more nervousness."

— Dalai Lama XIV

"The way you overcome shyness is to become so wrapped up in something that you forget to be afraid."

— LADY BIRD JOHNSON

Fear is a powerful and primitive human emotion. It alerts us to danger, and it was critical in keeping our ancestors alive. Fear can be divided into two responses: biochemical and emotional. The biochemical reaction is universal, while the emotional response is highly individual. The psychological condition of fear is removed from any concrete and real immediate danger. It comes in many forms: unease, worry, anxiety, nervousness, tension, dread, phobia, and so on. This kind of psychological fear is always of something that might happen, not of something happening now. You are in the

"Fear is a question. What are you afraid of and why? Our fears are a treasure house of self-knowledge if we explore them."

– MARILYN FRENCH

here and now while your mind is in the future. This creates an anxiety gap. And if you are identified with your mind and have lost touch with the power and simplicity of the now, that anxiety gap will be your constant companion. You can always cope with the present moment, but you cannot deal with something that is only a mind projection. You cannot cope with the future.

Theories of emotion have a long history, and perennial questions remain. How many emotions are there? Are emotions discrete or dimensional? What is their function? Which ones are unique to humans? Historically, much of the work has been done in philosophy and psychology with an almost exclusive focus on humans. More than a century ago, psychologist William James already envisioned emotions as corresponding to specific psychophysiological patterns in the body. However, he recognised that each instance of emotion might have a different pattern. Indeed, finding reliable psychophysiological patterns that would classify emotion categories — for example, happiness versus sadness — is an idea for which there has been little empirical support. Nowadays, this picture has been transposed into the brain, and the debate remains alive. Are there specific brain systems for happiness, for fear, for anger, and sadness?

Because of its phantom nature and despite elaborate defence mechanisms, the ego is very vulnerable and insecure, and it sees itself as constantly under threat. This is the case even if the ego is outwardly very confident. Now, remember that an emotion is the body's reaction to your mind.

"It is not failure itself that holds you back; it is the fear of failure that paralyzes you."

— BRIAN TRACY

What message is the body receiving continuously from the ego, the false, mind-made self? Danger, I am under threat. And what is the emotion generated by this continuous message? Fear, of course.

Fear has many causes. Fear of loss, fear of failure, fear of being hurt, and so on, but ultimately all fear is the ego's fear of death, of annihilation. To the ego, death is always just around the corner. In this mind-identified state, fear of death affects every aspect of your life.

For example, even a seemingly trivial and "normal" thing as the compulsive need to be right in an argument and make the other person wrong – defending the mental position with which you have identified – is due to the fear of death. If you identify with a mental position and you are wrong, your mind-based sense of self is seriously threatened with annihilation. So, the ego cannot afford to be incorrect. To be wrong is to die. Wars have been fought over this, and countless relationships have broken down.

Once you have dis-identified from your mind, whether you are right or wrong makes no difference to your sense of self at all, so the forcefully compulsive and deeply unconscious need to be correct, which is a form of violence, will no longer be there. You can state clearly and firmly how you feel or what you think, but there will be no aggressiveness or defensiveness about it. Your sense of self is then derived from a deeper and truer place within yourself, not from the mind.

Watch out for any defensiveness within yourself. What are you defending? A false identity, an image in your mind, a fictitious entity?

By making this pattern conscious, by witnessing it, you dis-identify from it. In the light of your consciousness, the unconscious habit will then quickly dissolve.

This is the end of all arguments and power games, which are so corrosive to relationships. Power over others is weakness disguised as strength. Real power is within, and it is available to you now.

Fear is commonly thought to have adaptive functions in both cognition and behavioural response. Unlike reflexes and fixed-action patterns, the relationship between stimuli and behaviours mediated by fear is highly flexible and context-dependent (see the section below on the modulation of fear). This flexibility is part of what distinguishes emotions. They are 'decoupled reflexes', central states more akin to personality traits and dispositions. One feature that highlights this is the highly diverse yet integrated sets of psychophysiological, cognitive, and behavioural changes that all serve as indices of a central state of fear. Yet one of the most prominent behavioural aspects of fear in humans remains of debated functional significance: facial expressions of fear. There is vast literature regarding emotional facial expressions (probably the most commonly used class of stimulus in human studies of emotion) with strong claims regarding their cultural universality or relativity and their biological primacy or social construction.

Causes of fear

Even though this book is about fearless public speaking. It is always essential to understand the concept of "fear".

Fear is incredibly complex. Some fears may be because of experiences or trauma, while others may represent a fear of something else entirely, such as losing control. Still, other fears may occur because they cause physical symptoms, such as fear of heights, which can make you feel dizzy and sick. Experience is one major component of fear. This aetiological view of fear makes meaning out of negative life experiences from either the environment, teachers, trauma, peers, and sometimes the personality of the individual in question. It is interesting to note that as babies, we have only two fears: loud noise and falling. However, these two develop and morph into complex expressions depending on our experiences.

Common fears

- Agoraphobia: fear of open spaces
- Social phobias
- Acrophobia: fear of heights
- Pteromerhanophobia: fear of flying
- Claustrophobia: fear of enclosed spaces

- Cynophobia: fear of dogs
- Ophidiophobia: fear of snakes
- Trypanophobia: fear of needles
- Astraphobia: fear of storms
- Entomophobia: fear of insects

Chapter Exercise

Write down the reasons you have stage fright or fear speaking publicly.

1 ....

2 ....

3 ....

4 ....

5 ....

6 ....

7 ....

8 ....

9 ....

10 ....

"Fear of public speaking can include fear of forgetting your words, fear of being judged, fear of difficult questions or all of these."

— IBRAHIM MUSTAPHA

Stage fright cripples you when it is time to act. The world is your stage, and you must be prepared to take advantage of that to sell yourself. After discovering your why, it is natural to feel afraid, especially if you are not ready to take that leap. Stage fright can make a person anxious, sweaty, and uncomfortable while addressing others.

5 Tips To Know If You Are Experiencing Stage Fright

If you are unsure of what stage fright feels like, answer these questions with yes or no answers:

Chapter Exercise II

1. Do you experience dry mouth and tight throat?

Yes............No..........

"You are not being judged, the value of what you are bringing to the audience is being judged."

— SETH GODIN

Experiencing dry mouth and tight throat is a symptom that can cause some speakers to speak slowly and frightfully. The tightness of the throat is also another symptom associated with dryness in the mouth. If this happens to you, take sips of water and repeat positive affirmations to yourself.

2. Do you experience sweaty and cold hands?

    Yes............No..........

Sweaty and cold hands can make the person feel less inspired to make hand gestures, which can ultimately make the speaker appear rigid. If you always sweat and feel a coldness in your palms, then you are experiencing stage fright. If this happens to you, go over your notes and assure yourself that you are in control.

3. Do you experience nausea and an uneasy feeling in the abdomen?

    Yes............No..........

Nausea is a common symptom of stage fright that affects individuals about to speak to a crowd. This uncomfortable feeling can cause the person to feel less confident about continuing with the speech and ultimately shatter the person's presentation style. If this happens to you, ask for a break to catch your breath.

4. Do you experience changes in vision?

   Yes............No..........

This symptom usually affects those who speak to a large crowd. If this happens to you, calm down and take occasional sips of water.

5. Do you experience rapid breathing?

   Yes............No..........

Rapid breathing happens when you are about to speak. This fear is natural. Catch your breath and let it pass.

Causes of Stage Fright and How to Overcome Them

1. Self-consciousness

"Always be yourself and have faith in yourself. Do not go out and look for a successful personality and try to duplicate it."

— BRUCE LEE

Self-consciousness happens when a person is excessively aware of his/her abilities and flaws, so it leads to increased levels of stress. You will do better when you are less self-conscious of yourself as you plan to speak on stage, at a presentation, maybe at a job interview or any other speaking engagement where you'd be expected to present at your best.

2. Fear of making mistakes

The fear of errors is one of the significant causes of stage fright. We keep wondering, what if I don't speak well? What if I forget my introduction? What if I fail to impress the audience? These are speculative questions about things that may never happen, so when you worry about them, you increase your stage anxiety. Stop Worrying and go all out. Give it your very best and pick yourself up each time you think you've made a mistake and try again.

3. Past failures in public speaking

Sometimes, stage fright could result from past public speaking failures, which makes us feel like the same thing might happen again. If an individual doesn't let go of such omissions or thoughts of failing, they will struggle with stage fright for a long time. Let go. A page from my life would help drive home this point. For me, the fear of public speaking almost wrecked my professional career as I was starting as a young trial advocate. I remember it all so clearly, almost as if it happened a few hours ago.

On September 1, 2000, I made my maiden appearance as a barrister and solicitor of the Supreme Court of Nigeria. I had always dreamt of being "the trial attorney" like Matlock, a TV fictional character that aired in the late 70s and early 80s. Maybe you would relate more to Ross and Harvey from *Suits*. In any case, I wanted to be a magnificent attorney — the only one you would ever need.

You know reality and dreams don't always tally, right? They are akin to two bulls locking horns and pushing for territory. At least, that is how I see it most days. I didn't see it this way when I was a child. I thought as a child and believed everything I saw, and it made me feel good.

Alas! Life happened. A rude awakening occurred, and life as I came to know and expect shifted a bit out of the rose-coloured frame I was used to.

On that day, as my case was called, due to my intense fear as I stood up to address the judge at the Lagos State High Court, my mind sat down! Yes, my mind didn't follow me in this formal presentation it considered a charade. I completely blanked out. My mind was uncooperative, and the nerves set in. I had forgotten my lines because of my nerves. A ball of yarn being kicked around by a cat was better than I was – it was moving – but I wasn't! I could hear everything as loud as a thousand explosions, and the sound of my heart racing filled my ears with doom.

The silence in the minute I took to remember my lines dragged on into eternity.

Soon I began my speech after I recalled some of my lines. "May it please my Lord, I am Mr Aniche, counsel, I represent the claimant. This is a Breach of Contract case. I can confirm the four requirements of a valid contract were present in this agreement, Offer, Acceptance, Consideration, and the Intention to Enter into a Valid Legal Relationships."

As soon as I released the words, my mouth went dry, butterflies congregated in my stomach, and my heart pounded. Boom! Boom! Boom!

Cold sweat ran down my forehead. My hands were shaking as if I was in a vibrating plate, and then my right knee shuddered. Soon, my left knee joined in synchronisation.

I was disgraced, dispirited, and despondent.

I was not "the articulate advocate" I had hoped and dreamed about for years. I was a lame duck!

The following week, I was forced to go to court again by my principal. It was to move for a motion for an adjournment. Due to my intense fear when my case was called, I could not stand this time I docked. I was lucky my client was not in court because it would have been a disaster for me.

"I have not failed. I've simply discovered 10,000 ways that don't work."

— THOMAS EDISON

For ten long years, I didn't dare set foot in a courtroom. My dream was gone. I was no longer living my dreams but my fears. Fear became my reality. I coped with my fears through avoidance rather than facing it head-on. Professionally, I missed out on opportunities to grow in my career. My fear of public speaking was a micro-cosm of the entirety of my fear of failing.

But on January 1, 2010, I resolved to tackle my fear of pub-lic speaking. Yes, I took that long to come to this resolution because I was avoiding it.

I thought I could take the shortcut by paying a hypnotist in cen-tral London to banish my fear forever in October 2010. He only managed to put me to sleep for two hours! That was the most expensive sleep I have ever slept because I paid him £250 to sleep on a chair, not even on a bed. I still marvel when I think about that day at his office and his promises to banish my fear of speaking forever and my desperation to get rid of the anxiety so much, that I handed over to someone two hundred and fifty quid to put me to sleep!

If you were wondering, it didn't work. I only slept away the fear for the two hours as I was already exhausted when I got to his office after a long day at work. It returned the moment my eyes were open. Right now, I still think about how gullible

"All the great speakers were bad speakers at first."

– RALPH WALDO EMERSON

I was in trying to look for the short route to success. Despite all my disappointments, I didn't stop pushing to overcome my fears. I soldiered on and tried different methods. I read books and attended seminar after seminar. I studied great speakers in a bid to get a glimpse into their minds and how it worked. I joined Toastmasters, a non-profit educational organisation that teaches public speaking and leadership skills through a worldwide network of clubs. Toastmasters played a part in my journey to becoming a fearless speaker.

Also, I did several other court trial and communication skills training with the National Institute of Trial Advocacy, USA. NITA is the premier advocacy training institution in the world. I employed private coaches, consultants and even a part-time judge to assist me in my quest to become an effective and articulate communicator because I knew the benefit of speaking with eloquence and poise was enormous.

When I became much more confident as a speaker, opportunities opened up for me, I became an accomplished trial advocate in the courtroom arguing family cases in the higher courts of England and Wales because I had become a Solicitor Advocate in the superior court of England and Wales. I won several cases brought before very demanding Judges. I wouldn't have won these cases If I hadn't become an articulate advocate.

Opportunities continued to open for me as I was appointed as a seasonal lecturer, teaching mooting and communication skills at the University of Canterbury Christ Church. In addition, and very recently as a speaker for Central Law Training, one of the biggest Legal Training Organisation, training lawyers in the United Kingdom.

Finally, my dream to coach others became a reality. I now lecture and coach small business owners, professionals and in many cases in front of an audience of between 100 to 500 people or more.

My 20 years' experience of learning the ropes to become a competent and professional speaker taught me some proper lessons which I have systematised in this book. I have also highlighted some ways to grow as a speaker, which I discovered most self-help books did not contain.

My odyssey has been long and arduous. Yet, despite all of this breakthrough, at times, I still have some niggling phobia for speaking in public the difference now is that I know it is okay to 'feel the fear and do it anyway', as Susan Jeffers made me realise in her book with the same title. The speakers you look up to and admire also face the same problem you do; the difference lies in how they handle and perceive them. Perception is critical in this public speaking journey and everything in life.

According to Mark Twain, "There are two types of speakers, those that are nervous and those that are liars." All professional speakers will agree that some level of nervousness before a great speech or presentation is normal. Any speaker who tells you they don't feel nervous before and during presentations is not being truthful. By the way, it is fine to be nervous before a speech or a presentation as long as you positively channel your energy in the right direction, you will deliver a fantastic speech or presentation.

To reduce any form of nervousness, you need to stay clear of the following:

a. Insufficient preparation

Sometimes we don't prepare well enough; hence, the reason we feel pressure and tension, which leads to stage fright. For example, when a speaker decides to prepare his / her presentation at the last moment, it is very likely they will experience nervousness due to a lack of adequate preparation. In order to avert this, the speaker must prepare sufficiently by doing the relevant research that would enable them to know their subject matter properly.

b. Wrong comparisons

> *"Expect the best. Prepare for the worst. Capitalize on what comes."*
>
> — ZIG ZIGLAR

Some people experience stage fright because of a lack of originality; they try to copy others and put too much pressure on themselves. The seasoned speakers you try to copy also had the challenges you have now, so when you try to imitate them, you build fear within you. Being afraid is natural. However, you need to surmount this stage fright and challenge yourself to do better. Don't allow this little element to take over your mindset. You must recognise the fear when you feel it and seek ways to manage it. It is okay for you to be nervous, and you should know that you are NOT alone! The most exceptional communicators also suffered from fear, but they overcame it; you can too. The most important thing is for you not to be so hard on yourself by expecting instant perfection after a few tries.

C. Insufficient Practice

Another reason you struggle with stage fright is that you don't speak or practice regularly. When you get used to speaking frequently, the stage fright will gradually phase out, and you will be much more confident. Give yourself time to practice and get better. Be patient with the process, and you will see yourself improve. Remember that your audience isn't aware that you are nervous even when you feel anxious. Stage fright escalates when we think people *know* that we are afraid. Your audience only sees what you show them. Show confidence, and what goes on in your mind won't matter.

The above points will help you on your journey to overcoming stage fright.

We have just completed the foundational aspect of this book by considering the significant issues of stage fright, which prevents some people from speaking fearlessly. This is crucial as it helps put many things into perspective.

Public speaking is an art and a process that entails physical, emotional, and mental capabilities. But for you to achieve a great psychological state, you must be physically prepared.

Stage fright and anxiety are two of the most typical issues people deal with regarding public speaking. If you have ever experienced stage fright, you will agree that it is nerve-wracking, and it can affect you tremendously.

5 'D's To Conquer Stage Fright

"Let thy speech be better than silence, or be silent."

– Dionysius Of Halicarnassus

There are some vocal relaxation techniques and practices that help you deal with stage fright. Such methods can be repeatedly done until you feel very confident about speaking.

1. Derive joy from positive visualisation

"Visualize yourself, giving the entire speech as a controlled, confident speaker."

— Ibrahim Mustapha

Positive visualization speaks of your ability to mentally visualize the outcome of your speech even before you give it. This technique helps you have positive expectations for your presentation, and this will boost your performance. You can practice positive visualisation weeks before your speech and a few hours to the address. Imagine connecting with the audience and getting positive feedback, then hold on to this image in your mind while speaking.

2. Ditch the pacing

Pacing increases tension, especially before and while talking. There is a difference between pacing in anxiety and walking while talking to make a point. Excessively pacing is often a sign of tension and stress, which you must fight off. Whenever you feel the temptation to walk, stand still, take a short speaking pause, and then continue.

3. Don't be late

Yes, as minor as this may seem, it is a deal-breaker. If you arrive late, you will feel tensed up and try to make up for your lateness by rushing your speech. But an early arrival gets you settled in and enables you to practice the other pre-speaking activities that will keep you calm. Sometimes lateness may occur due to circumstances beyond your control, so don't be so hard on yourself. But you must intentionally strive to ensure that you arrive early enough to become familiar with the environment and practise positive visualisation there. Don't be late!

4. Drench yourself in rest

Most of the time, stage fright could be because of a lack of rest before speaking in public. So instead of showing up relaxed, you show up tired and ready to rush through it. Getting adequate rest before your speech contributes to building self-confidence, and a confident person wouldn't become a victim of stage fright.

5. Deep breathing exercises help

Before speaking, use warm-up methods that will help calm your nerves and keep anxiety off. Warm-up habits vary for speakers, but the most prominent one that is very helpful for all speakers, especially those that want to be fearless, is deep breathing. Deep breathing is a warm-up routine that helps in keeping you calm and in control before speaking. When taking deep breaths, remember to feel relaxed because that is the whole idea in the first place. Don't take deep breaths thinking about the crowd you are about to face; it will make you feel tensed up. Take deep breaths, thinking about absolutely nothing!

7 Tips to Help You Make the Gradual Shift from Fright to Might

Moving from fright to might (which is the next stage to be discussed in the next chapter) is gradual. To move from this stage, you need to build your skill while learning a couple of evergreen techniques like storytelling.

1. Tell Stories

Storytelling in public speaking is essential. This doesn't necessarily mean telling many stories. It means carrying your audience along in a conversational manner while applying the right life stories to drive home your point. You can deal with stage fright by sharing personal stories with your audience as you speak. People love it when there is a realistic connection to what is being said. But first, let us look at what storytelling is so we can distinguish it from what it's not. You have probably seen the term or heard it being thrown about in conversations, but do you understand what it means? What if I tell you that everything comprises stories? Yes, everything. There is a fat chance you haven't noticed this yet, but the moment you realise this, everything changes.

Here's an example. A body is found washed up on the shore, and the police try to identify the body. They go through dental records and several databases looking for a match. An autopsy is carried out to determine the likely cause of death – it is not acceptable to assume the person was killed just because the body was found close to water. Everything I detailed here is

> *"Don't worry. You'll find your message in your mess."*
>
> — RICHIE NORTON

something you have probably seen if you watch *NCIS* or any movie involving murder and police investigations. What are the chances of you not seeing any, anyway? Next to zero, right?

You may be wondering what point I am trying to make with this long-winded speech. Well, here it is: did you notice the story in what I narrated?

I am not referring to the death of a person or the involvement of law enforcement. Look closer. Have you seen it? Do you know why I said everything comprises stories?

"Effective communication is 20% what you know and 80% how you feel about what you know."

– Jim Rohn

The autopsy report is a story of everything that happened to the body of the victim. Your body is a map of sorts; everything you have eaten is archived, your cells encode the history of your lineage, and every vaccination you have taken to this point can be traced in your body. But you would not know how to decode this information unless you have the necessary tools and an understanding to go with it. Storytelling is implementing narrative and facts to communicate to your audience. This simple definition of storytelling holds so much weight and can be stretched to everything in the universe. When water boils, it is telling you a story about its state. When your stomach rumbles, your belly is preaching the tale of hunger. When shooting stars cross through the sky, it is telling you a story of the business in the sky.

"Perfection, in the form of a flawless stream of words delivered with cool composure, is never as persuasive as realness. An impassioned but imperfect speech, which shows you care too much to hide flaws, is far more compelling."

— CHARLOTTE BEERS

Stories stimulate imagination and passion and create a sense of community among listeners and tellers alike. Some stories are factual, and some are embellished or improvised to explain the core message, or to explain the core message better. While this definition is specific, stories resemble a variety of things.

Storytelling is an art form, as old as time and has a place in every culture and society. Why? Because stories are a universal language that everyone — regardless of heritage, dialect, or hometown — can understand.

"The more strikingly visual your presentation is, the more people will remember it. And more importantly, they will remember you."

– PAUL ARDEN

Telling a story is a lot like painting a picture with words; you know the saying, *"A picture is worth a thousand words."* Perhaps everyone on this planet can tell a story and weave intricate tales together to pull out various emotions from their audience. Yet, certain people have fine-tuned their storytelling skills. These people are usually dubbed storytellers and can be found putting out content on the net or working on behalf of brands, businesses, and organisations that need their stories told. There is a segment of these storytellers who are popularly called marketers or public relations professionals because of their primary job description. Storytellers go by different names and can be found in almost every situation. Every member of an organization can tell a story. But before we get into how to, let's talk about the reason we tell stories. As Simon Sinek would say, "Let's talk about the *why* of storytelling."

There are several reasons we tell stories, and they range from inward realization to pushing outward expectations. Stories play a vital role when we want to communicate, brag, sell, educate, or even threaten someone or a group of people. Stories can instil fear and cripple an entire generation or society from moving and taking affirmative action. Stories and their retelling can also liberate because they can be the catalyst for change in behaviour or change in how people view life.

But my focus now is to show you why we would always choose storytelling over other data conveyor methods, like a bulleted list or a PowerPoint presentation. I want to show you why stories get us to feel things differently while passing on the same information data-driven presentations contain. Let's face it, most presentations make you fall asleep anyway, but you sit straight and drink in everything that is served up by a good storyteller.

Why do you think that is?

Here's why:

Stories motivate

Tapping into people's emotions and baring, both the good and evil, is how stories inspire and motivate. Motivation then evolves into action that changes the narrative or the course of history. Stories give life to a brand and make us human. We remember the deeds of people, like Alexander Graham Bell, Ernest Hemingway, and Abraham Lincoln, because of the stories woven around them; their deeds became a piece of clothing that gave them flesh and made them tangible and larger than life. When brands get authentic and transparent, it brings them down-to-earth and helps consumers connect with them and rally people around them. Stories – good stories – bring a form of goodwill to brands and individuals and foster loyalty; building a strong narrative around your brand humanizes and markets your business.

Stories bring unity

Stories are a universal language of sorts; they encode the feelings, hopes, and aspirations of society. We resonate with the tale of the hero and the underdog. We understand heartbreak all too well. As humans or beings of higher intelligence, we process emotions and can share feelings of despair, anger, elation, and hope.

"The success of your presentation will be judged not by the knowledge you send but by what the listener receives."

– LILLY WALTERS

In a world divided by a plethora of things, stories bring people together and create a sense of community. Despite your societal background, political preferences, or religion; stories cut through all of that and hit the nail on the head. It is the thread that makes ends meet and a leveller of differences. Stories connect us through the way we feel and respond to them despite our glaring differences. Stories have no skin tone; they are neutral and all-inclusive at the same time.

Sharing what we feel and hold dear in a story gives even the most diverse people a sense of commonality and community.

In short, stories make us human.

Storytelling always involves the presentation of a narrative. There are other art forms that also present stories, but storytelling as an art unto itself goes about it differently. Every culture has its definition of story, and what is recognised as a story in one situation may not be accepted as one in another. Some situations call for spontaneity and repetitions, while others require digression and heavy use of the imagination.

Just look all around you, and you will notice the world that has taken shape because of stories. Comic conventions are an example of a world that has grown and will continue to grow, branch out, and flourish because stories form its heart. People from all over the world and various walks of life gather all because of this single thread that binds and transmits feelings, hopes, and aspirations, which are attributes we understand all too well, even if we can't put them into words.

"I've learned that people will forget what you said, people will forget what you did, but people will never forget how you made them feel."

— MAYA ANGELOU

Stories simplify complex concepts

We have all been there at one point or another: the cold confusion of grappling a new idea/topic. We have experienced the overwhelming weight of trying to understand something despite having the information needed in front of our eyes. Stories provide a way around that. Cast your mind back to all the times' simple stories made you understand a concept or deepen your love and understanding for an idea. It may be a preacher breaking down religious text by sliding in story bits, a teacher explaining a complex mathematical concept by relating it to everyday life, an epiphany hitting you between the eyes while watching a movie, or the way a speaker connects the dots between disciplines through simple storytelling devices.

"Storytelling is the most powerful way to put ideas into the world today."

— ROBERT McKEE

Stories aid the simplification of complex messages. They also solidify abstract concepts. Stories take intangible concepts and formless ideas as raw materials that become concrete ideas through its relationship with everyday life. The strength of stories lies in its malleability and seamless adaptability to every situation.

As an example, notice how top companies advertise or explain their product to the general public; technical jargon is mostly relegated to the back burner while everyday language is employed. You would be hard-pressed to find an advert by

Samsung, Google, or Apple that favours the use of technical language over relatable, everyday speech. Why? It's quite simple when you think about it. Although they build these products using technical parlance, most people are unfamiliar with it. They can't sell or explain their importance to everyday consumers using that same language. And this is where stories come in as a bridge that links both worlds.

What Makes a Good Story

We just covered a lot of ground on why we tell stories, but what makes these stories excellent and worth mentioning? You should know and understand the anatomy of a good story as this helps you put together one whenever the opportunity arises. Good or bad is entirely subjective and relative to an individual's taste. But specific components must be involved for a story to go from average to exceptional. These components make for a memorable storytelling experience and will have your audience eating from your hand. Master them, and your public speaking prowess will more than double.

- **Entertaining:** This should not even be a surprise. Good stories keep the listener/reader glued to their seat in anticipation of what comes next. There is a precarious balance of suspense and information in a good story that makes it irresistible.

- **Educational:** Curiosity does not always kill the cat. A perfectly good story brings to life the curiosity in your audience and adds to their knowledge repository. Always strive to bring new and fresh knowledge to your stories and apply the same concept to your presentation.

- **Universal:** Good stories are relatable because they have drawn from the wealth of feelings and experiences common to humanity. Good stories are an integral part of what has been and is being felt by humans.

- **Organized:** The telling of good stories has a structure that doesn't always follow the same format but is easily recognisable when examined. The classic tale of boy meets girl can be told and has been approached in different forms through the years. We see this in *Romeo and Juliet, Tristan and Isolde,* and right down to *Titanic.* Good stories always follow a path that makes for a memorable experience and not always easy consumption and deconstruction.

- **Memorable:** Good stories are memorable. They latch on to our emotions and bleed them to live. The lifeblood of a story lies in how much emotion it can draw out from the audience as that is the secret of being memorable. The more an audience sees itself and resonates with what is being presented equals the chances of the story not being forgotten.

"Tell me and I forget. Teach me and I remember. Involve me, and I learn."

– BENJAMIN FRANKLIN

An example of a fearless speaker that has mastered the art of story-telling and reels you in with every word is Les Brown. Les knows precisely how to balance these elements, which is the main reason he connects so well with his audience and engages them in a way that very few speakers can. He is impressive at tugging the emotions of his audience and tying in whatever he is speaking on with the right words and emotions.

But regardless of the story, you want to convey to your audience; three core concepts constitute a good story. These concepts are sometimes called by different names or further broken down, but the essence has been retained here for the sake of comprehension, assimilation, and mastery. The three important concepts/attributes are presented here:

Characters

Every story feature at least one character. I mean, we all know this from watching TV as children. We root for the protagonist and recognize and frown at the antagonist. Every story has at least one character because stories require something/someone to be the subject or object; we need a centre to tell meaningful stories. The character is the key to bringing your audience to the story. The character serves as a tie-in for your audience and as a source of vicarious living; this component is the bridge between you, the storyteller, and the audience. Painting your character in a way that is relatable and helps the audience see themselves in the character's shoes would better help you elicit emotion and action. Character development cannot be overemphasised if you want to present characters that are real and believable.

Conflict

Conflict is the spice of stories. Without conflict, stories would be stale and boring. As humans, we like listening to stories that tell of the adventure of the human spirit: the long winding road of hardship that leads to victory. We feel oddly at ease when we hear the challenges of life and eventual happiness. We are a people that strangely don't enjoy the sweet part of things unless we are shown the bitter components. Stories of conflict elicit emotions and connect the audience through relatable experiences. If there's no conflict in your story, it's likely not a story. What morals are to be gleaned from a tale that has no conflict? What would be the point of telling a story that has only happy incidents and is void of triumph?

Resolution

Every good story has a closing or a resolution, but it doesn't always have to be a good one. You shouldn't bend over to give your audience the ending they want, but you should provide them with one they deserve. What do I mean by a resolution they deserve? Well, you are taking their time to convey knowledge, so you must lend yourself to whatever path would cater to this need. A good ending doesn't always have to be happy.

Did Romeo and Juliet end on a happy note? Are there people still talking about this tale in this era? See my point? The power of the story doesn't lie in happy endings but in giving a well-deserved finish. Your story's resolution should wrap up the story within the context and world built around these characters and conflicts, then leave your audience with their thoughts. Your job is done at this point because you have served the story by conveying the core message that needed to be transmitted.

The Storytelling Process

Now, after talking about what comprises a good story, we can move on and talk about the storytelling process. As with anything in life that stands the test of time, a procedure is involved, and storytelling is no different. Storytelling, like other forms of art, requires skill, vision, and creativity.

Practising is also an essential factor. No one becomes a good storyteller by idly sitting in or by admiring storytellers that have mastered the craft. Storytelling requires doing; you must get knee-deep in the trenches and bleed out mistakes until you can push out only great stories.

Malcolm Gladwell's 10,000-hour principle comes to play here. If you are unfamiliar with this principle, pick up his book *Outliers.* For those curious, here is a summary: Malcolm's research shows that to be considered a professional in any field, one must have invested 10,000 hours into the said field. Sounds unbelievable, right? I know! But the data in his research is undeniable.

"When speaking in public, your message - no matter how important - will not be effective or memorable if you don't have a clear structure."

— PATRICIA FRIPP

"It's much easier to be convincing if you care about your topic. Figure out what's important to you about your message and speak from the heart.

– NICHOLAS BOOTHMAN

Painters, sculptors, sketch artists, and potters all follow their creative process when producing their art. Practice helps you know where to start, the route to developing your vision, and how to perfect this religion of practice over time. This same principle goes for storytelling and speech. You need practice if you ever want to improve and show the fruits of your labour.

Why is this process necessary? As a brand or an organisation, you are more than likely to have a large boat of messages, facts, and figures ready to go into the story you want to present. The same applies to you as a speaker, because you have all this data swimming around in your head and desk with no idea about where to start. You must have realised by now that knowing where to start is as important as knowing the components of a good story. So, in the upcoming section, I will address the checks you should go through so you can piece together the data you have and present a compelling and cohesive story.

2. Know your audience

You know the saying by that famous philosopher, "Know thyself?" Good. Now, turn this outward and know your audience. What group of people would benefit from the story you have to tell? Who wants to hear your story? Who will benefit and respond to the strongest? Where

"Picture yourself in a living room having a chat with your friends. You would be relaxed and comfortable talking to them, the same applies when public speaking."

— SIR RICHARD BRANSON

do they hang out? How can you find them? What financial level do they occupy? Can you immediately recognise them during a conversation? To create a compelling story, you must understand your audience.

Before you put pen to paper or sit down to type, carry out research on your target audience and their proclivities. Going through this process will get you acquainted, and up to speed with the category, you want to reach. You will suddenly understand the people who will find your message relevant. As a speaker well on the way to becoming fearless, knowing your audience is as important as knowing your strengths and weaknesses and playing within the set boundary.

> *"The royal road to a man's heart is to talk to him about the things he treasures most."*
>
> — DALE CARNEGIE

Knowing your audience will also provide valuable direction for the next few steps as you build the foundation of your story. You'll need to pay careful attention at this stage as it is crucial to your success and the response you may be aiming for; failure to understand your audience will definitely lead to many complications and some awkwardness when you say things that are sensitive due to ignorance. Remember that what one group considers funny may not translate as funny to another group, which means carrying out due diligence is imperative.

3. Know your why

Some call this purpose: the driving force behind why you do what you do. But here, let us call it your why. Every company that has succeeded and shown considerable influence in the sector they occupy knows and understands their why.

"If you can't explain it simply, you don't understand it well enough."

— ALBERT EINSTEIN

Every captain of an industry that has weathered the storm of change and still retains the piece of land they laid claim to know their why. You can't go the distance without understanding this; you can only go so far before you crash or retreat to re-evaluate your mission.

Whether your story is one page or twenty pages, or your presentation is only 20 minutes long, it should have a core message.

Similar to the foundation of a building, it must be established before moving forward. Is your story all about selling a product or calling people to rally around a cause? Are you planning a presen-

"The most valuable of all talents is never using two words when one will do."

— THOMAS JEFFERSON

tation to help you seal a deal? Maybe you are about to pitch to an executive, and you don't know where to start. Your why is exactly where you need to put down your flag. To help define this, summarise your story in six to ten words and build everything else around this. If you can't do that, you have no core message.

"Communication without clarity is noise. Speak with purpose, and you'll propel your audience to take massive action towards a journey of self-improvement."

— FARSHAD ASL

And if a core message is absent, what else is there to say? Why give a speech or stand behind a lectern to address people? Find your why and make it the core of everything – you don't always have to spell it out and write from this place of solid understanding and thorough love of what you do.

4. What do you want to share?

Remember when I said to find your why? Good. I believe you have done that. If so, this part will be easy. Not all stories are created equal. I am not referencing *Animal Farm,* but you can think of it that way. You must understand the texture of your story and determine what kind of story you want to tell and the feeling you want to leave your audience with.

"Communication without clarity is noise. Speak with purpose, and you'll propel your audience to take massive action towards a journey of self-improvement."

— Farshad Asl

This will help you determine how you'll weave your story and what objective you're pursuing. I am going to introduce you to the key points to guide you through this process. Every point helps you tailor that story if it matches the objective. The 5 points are as follows:

i. **Incite action:** If this is your objective, avoid excessive, exaggerated detail so your audience can focus on the action or change that your story encourages. Your story should describe a successful action completed in the past and explain how listeners might implement the same kind of change.

ii. **Convey values:** Tell a story that taps into known territories and characterization. Present situations that will show how it relates to everyday life. This is especially important when discussing values that some people might not agree with or understand.

iii. **Foster collaboration:** Tell a story that moves readers to discuss and share your story with others. Use a situation or experience that others can relate to and would be excited to talk about.

iv. **Talk about yourself:** Tell a story that encapsulates your life, mistakes and all. Listeners enjoy following the story of a speaker as this experiential knowledge would help them avoid the same mistake.

v. **Educate:** Present a story that features a trial-and-error experience so readers can learn about a problem and how a solution was discovered and applied. Discuss alternative solutions and methods to achieve these solutions.

5. Know your objective

Your objective and call-to-action are similar, but your call-to-action will establish the action you'd like your audience to take after reading.

What exactly do you want your audience to do after they listen to you? Do you want them to donate money, subscribe to a newsletter, take a course, or buy a product? Outline this alongside your objective to make sure they line up.

For example, if your objective is to foster community or collaboration, your call-to-action might be to "Tap the share button below."

Choose a medium & own it

Stories can take many shapes and forms. Some stories are read, some are watched, and others are listened to. Your chosen story medium depends on your type of story as well as resources. In this instance, we are focusing on storytelling as it relates to public speaking.

Here are the different ways you can tell your story.

- **Written story** is told primarily through books, blog posts, or articles. These stories are mostly text, and sometimes include images that aid in the explanation of the text. Written stories are by far the most affordable and attainable method of storytelling as it only requires either a pen and paper or a word processor. Your

"Designing a presentation without an audience in mind is like writing a love letter and addressing it: To Whom It May Concern."

— Ken Haemer

speech/presentation will start from this stage before moving on to be consumed by the public.

- **Spoken story** is told in person. This is the type of story that touches on the core of this book. Spoken stories show up in a presentation, speech, or panel session. TED talks are popular forms of spoken stories and have been used to transmit crucial information. Because of their real-time, unedited nature, spoken stories require more practice and skill to convey messages and elicit emotions out of an audience. Public speaking is a different kettle of fish for telling stories, and it takes a considerable time for some people to be comfortable enough in their skins to address a sea of faces.

- **Audio story** is spoken aloud but recorded, and this sets it apart from the spoken story. Audio stories usually follow the route of podcasts and audiobooks, which can be provided on a subscription basis. It is quite cheap to produce and maintain this form of storytelling, and it helps you practice your public speaking. Most public speakers follow this stream right after they begin to garner followers.

- **Digital story** is told through a wide range of media, which includes but isn't limited to animation, games, and video. This type of story is the most preferred form of storytelling for transmitting and painting emotionally charged stories. As a fearless public speaker, you can employ the power of digital stories by making use of the media to reach a wider audience.

Get crafting is achieved when you sit down and draw from the inspiration in your mind and from your visual library. What is the message you want to convey? You should know your audience by now and what resonates with them. With your objective and

> *"If you don't use stories, audience members may enjoy your speech, but there is no chance they'll remember it."*
>
> – ANDRII SEDNIEV

core message at the ready, creating a compelling speech driven by storytelling should be easy. This step is more about putting flesh on the data you have collected about your audience and everything touched on so far. What you have in mind must come into this 3D space if its impact is to be felt; your audience is not minded readers. This is the point where the rubber meets asphalt in the creation process and should be treated as an essential step to public speaking. If you doubt your words at this point, you will probably waver on stage while presenting. Ensure you are certain, definite and feel strongly about anything you put down at this stage as it is a culmination and representation of yourself.

Share. Share. Share.

Creating a story is only half the battle. As a fearless public speaker, you must put out content that communicates the heart of your story while building your presence online. Depending on your chosen medium, share your story on social media and email those on your list. Although we are gearing these skills towards public speaking, don't forget to share and promote your story! Go live and speak to a virtual audience or get on a conference call and speak. Doing this as practice will reduce anxiety and boost your confidence. The videos you create can be as short as 5 minutes or more; the point is to get the word out about you while putting out a message to the world. Also, try making podcasts and interviewing people; the more you do this, the better you will become at speaking and human interaction. While preparing for a speech, connect the content of your address and what happened in real life. You will find that while sharing such stories, your audience's attention will be at a heightened level, and this will help you relax as you speak.

Also, rely on vivid images while using sensory details for your speech so you can give an audience pictures to work within their minds. Sometimes statements become annoying when you solely rely on words without mental stimulation. To calm your nerves, you can begin with a short, funny yet impactful story that is highly descriptive. This move will help you present a great speech and resonate with your audience.

Remember, don't forget to continually share share share your story with your audience at large.

6. Know when to speak and when to be silent

Martin Tupper once said, "Sometimes silence hath more eloquence than speech." Your speech is about an idea, but if the design doesn't resonate with your audience, the aim of the address will be lost. Know when to be silent and know when to let your speech resonate with your audience. By resonate, it means that the speech must mean something to the viewer intellectually and emotionally.

On an intellectual level, you will need to ensure that your audience understands the major points of your speech. It must make sense to them; otherwise, they will give you a round of applause and forget about what you said.

Emotions are also very crucial because they help people find meaning and hold on to such purpose while listening to a speech. Regardless of the niche or aspect, you will talk about, there can be an emotional aspect to it. Try to elicit emotions by asking distinctive questions and striking a connection between what you say and how it affects the audience in a personal way.

7. Clarity is Key

While speaking to a group of people, you become increasingly anxious when you are not clear about what you are saying. You will know that you haven't achieved clarity when the people you speak to look uninterested, confused, or bored. For you to avoid such negative instant feedback, you must ensure that you achieve clarity while speaking. Transparency is crucial for persuasiveness and articulation, especially when talking about something your audience needs convincing on. Speak directly on the topic at hand, don't move in circles, and avoid redundant and repetitive sentences. Your speech should be brief and impactful rather than lengthy and off point.

If you don't deal with stage fright and anxiety on a physical level, it will affect how you speak, and this will be visible to your audience. The people you talk to will most likely enjoy what you say when they sense you are confident. So be relaxed and show you appreciate what you are saying. The ideas shared in this chapter will help you fight off the impact of stage fright and anxiety while helping you maintain an excellent physical state as you speak. Moving from fright to might will be explained extensively in the next chapter.

The Competence Quadrant as a Fearless Speaker

Think of the competence quadrant as driving a car. Remember when you knew nothing about driving. You wondered how people could do it so effortlessly, and some even go on to drive on a competitive level. Think back to your first lesson when everything overwhelmed you, and the fear of running someone over got you worried. I am sure you broke into a cold sweat as every average human being would. In fact, what has happened is that the more you get behind the wheel, the more competent and subsequently more confident you become. This also applies to public speaking, the more you do it, the more confident and competent you'll become.

You discover suddenly, you want to go faster and cut through the traffic. With consistent practice, you will notice you've become confident on the wheel and all of a sudden you feel like you know all there is to know about it. You will be so proficient that it becomes an unconscious activity for you.

"To communicate, we must realize that we are all different in the way we perceive the world and use this understanding as a guide to our communication with others."

— TONY ROBBINS

The competence quadrant as a Fearless Speaker comprises four stages:

1. **The unconscious incompetence** is a situation where you are unaware of the skill of being able to speak fearlessly and your lack of proficiency.

2. **Unconscious competence** involves performing the art of fearless speaking, so it becomes second nature. This is the best stage to be as a fearless speaker and eloquent speaker

3. **Conscious incompetence,** this is being aware of the ability to speak without fear but at the same time being inproficient with the skill.

4. **Conscious competence** this is being able to speak fearlessly and at the same time being constrained by trying to be perfect by using all the well-known tools and techniques of Public Speaking

What stage are you in?

The benefits of being a competent/fearless speaker are enormous if you can move to the right quadrant.

As said earlier, public speaking is not a skill only used for speaking on stage but also can be used in the Marketing & Sales Profession, by Business Owners, by Professionals during interviews amongst other areas. It's a skill that will set you

Fearless Public Speaking apart and on how people perceive you generally. Learn to be confident as this can help you transform people's perceptions of you. An important thing to note here is this; the fear of public speaking cannot be entirely eradicated. As a speaker, you will continuously fret over your presentations and wonder if it is good enough. The solution will always be to go out there and deliver the message you have planned. Purpose always stabilises an individual and becomes the fuel that helps him/her overcome the hurdles thought of as impossible to surmount. Feel the fear but do it anyway should be your resolve. Always interpret fear as a sign of being on the right path. Fear should be the check signal that alerts you to the greatness within that is about to be revealed.

CHAPTER THREE

From Fright to Might: Converting Fear to Stage Might

Chapter Outline

"All we need to do is get those nervous butterflies in our stomachs flying in formation."

— Cathy Burnham Martin

The next stage in our Fearless Public Speaking System is moving to might! Moving from stage fright to stage might is possible once you have answered your why and knowing that stage fright is a natural element that can be overcome.

Stage fright is probably one of the scariest experience speakers will ever face because even after the speaking engagement, the memories remain in their mind.

"You don't have to be great to start, but you do have to start to be great."

— ZIG ZIGLAR

Stage fright is a massive problem for speakers, so if you have had a scary experience, it isn't something peculiar to you. According to Mark Twain, there are two types of speakers in the world:

1. The nervous speaker
2. The liar

1. The nervous speakers are those whose stage fright is openly portrayed to the audience because they haven't found a way to conceal it. The liars can cover this fear and make the most out of their speech despite being afraid.

Now we are all nervous speakers on the inside, but we must ensure that we do not let the fear out through stage fright.

What can we do? We can become liars who show the audience strength and confidence by speaking fearlessly.

2. Liars CONVERT nervous feelings into faith in themselves and make bold statements that help them overcome stage fright. Learn to take on this process of conversion by absorbing the key suggestions outlined in this chapter.

In this chapter, you will unearth steps that will help you convert your stage fright or anxiety into self-confidence and stage might. Before moving on to the steps, know there is no cure for fear of public speaking! You've got to accept your anxiety, convert it, and then get over it with every opportunity you've got to speak. The process of becoming a competent driver from your initial jittery stage to being comfortable on the wheel without having to think about what to do next is similar to learning to speak in public and becoming fearless.

7 Steps for Converting Stage Fright to Stage Might

1. Visualisation

"If it takes a lot of words to say what you have in mind, give it more thought."

— DENNIS ROTH

Visualization is a technique that can help you turn stage fright into stage might. Remember the words of William Shakespeare, which speaks of the absence of good or bad as only thinking makes it so. Whatever you visualize about the presentation is what you will get, so set aside thoughts of fear or failure. Visualize a successful speech, and you will have one. It isn't speculation. It is a fact.

2. Focus

"The way you overcome shyness is to become so wrapped up in something that you forget to be afraid."

— LADY BIRD JOHNSON

The speech aims to convey information to an audience. You are the conveyor of information, but the attention shouldn't be on you. Create a connection with your audience while ensuring that they are at the centre of the speech. When you use this strategy, you reduce the tension on yourself and feel even more relaxed.

3. Be Authentic

Some people in a bid to prepare for their speech watch the successful lectures of other people and copy their style. It is okay to be inspired, but don't copy because it makes it easier for you to lose your originality. It is okay for you to be vulnerable, but that doesn't mean you should become someone else. Always be yourself by expressing your authenticity while speaking.

"If something comes from your heart, it will reach the heart of your audience."

— FAWZIA KOOFI

Remember that the audience wants to connect with a relatable person, not a copy of someone else. You can be an original, you can be who you are, and you can show your uniqueness in the most excellent ways, so be authentic!

4. Be Positive

Regardless of how difficult you may think the speaking engagement will be, you must be positive about it. When you are positive, you will display might on stage because you already believe in yourself. Think about the excellence in your speech and how you intend to deliver flawlessly and then build inner positivity about the process.

"Expect the best. Prepare for the worst. Capitalize on what comes."

— ZIG ZIGLAR

As you do this, you will find that whenever you show up to speak, you are relaxed, smiling, and enjoying the process. Tension sets in when a person is negative about a speech, so don't give room for tension. Always think on the bright side whenever you speak to an audience.

5. Confidence

Acting confidently is also crucial in converting stage fright to stage might. The keyword here is "act" because it is understandable that you may not be confident at the time, but you shouldn't show that to your audience. You must

"Courage is what it takes to stand up and speak and to sit down and listen."

— WINSTON CHURCHILL

show your audience what you want them to see, which in this case should be confidence and poise. The more you do this, the easier it becomes for you to always express faith while speaking. After your first few speaking engagements, it will become natural for you to fearlessly speak because you've perfected this process over a long period of time.

6. Speaking slowly but clearly

Speak in a conversational tone that helps your audience grasp all you have to say. If you rush your words, you will struggle with staying confident, and if you are too slow, you will appear intimidating. When you speak too fast,

"Speak clearly, if you speak at all; carve every word before you let it fall."

— OLIVER WENDELL HOLMES

you do the same thing with your spoken words. You don't leave any long spaces of silence between phrases and sentences, thus making your listeners work too hard to understand what you are trying to say. Fearless and seasoned speakers, like Les Brown and Barrack Obama, are perfect examples of people that have mastered the art of being deliberately slow in their speech.

Remember the key problem: Listeners are intrinsically lazy. If you don't make it easy for them, they won't exert themselves to listen. Or if they do, they soon tire and tune you out. This is a serious problem for you, the speaker, because people draw conclusions about you based on how you speak, write, and think. We know now that attention is the fundamental difference between hearing and listening. Paying attention to what a speaker is saying requires intentional effort on the part of the listener.

"In presentations or speeches, less really is more."

— STEPHEN KEAGUE

Dr Nichols, credited with first researching the field of listening, observed, and noted that "Listening is hard work. It is characterized by faster heart action, quicker circulation of the blood, a small rise in bodily temperature." Consider that we can process information four times faster than a person speaks. Yet, tests of listening comprehension show the average person listens at only 25% efficiency.

A typical person can speak 125 words-per-minute, yet we can process up to three times faster, reaching as much as 500 words-per-minute. The poor listener grows impatient while the active listener uses the extra time to process the speaker's words, distinguish key points, and mentally summarise them.

Lord Chesterfield summed it up nicely when he said,

"The manner of your speaking is full as important as the matter, as more people have ears to be tickled than understandings to judge."

Science bears him out. There is clear evidence that fast talkers get credit for being smart, but they are also widely criticised behind their backs.

People interpret fast-talking as a sign of nervousness and a lack of self-confidence. Your fast-talking can make it appear that you don't think people want to listen to you or that what you have to say is not essential.

That you don't pause between phrases or at the end of sentences means that you're not taking in enough air to support your voice. Your breath stream becomes weak, and the words near the end of your utterance lack volume and clarity.

"Speak clearly, if you speak at all; carve every word before you let it fall."

— OLIVER WENDELL HOLMES

There are other consequences too. Rushing can ruin your diction. When you fly through your words, your tongue and lips can't keep up with your mind, so you drop important vowels and consonants, causing your listeners to miss your meaning.

And when they miss your meaning, most won't tell you they can't understand you. They may do so out of misplaced kindness or out of indifference to you and your message, but no matter the cause, you will have lost their attention.

So, here is an exercise that will cure you of your public speaking anxiety. It was given to me by Marian Rich, a voice and speech teacher in New York who worked with many famous actors to help them improve their vocal presence. The exercise will teach you that your voice is a wind instrument, and you must have ample air in your lungs to play it well.

Remember, always strive to strike a balance! Fear is okay; don't allow the anxiety to get the best of you by giving it too much attention. You must become conscious of your worries and discover ways to deal with them by using them positively. Implementing this will empower you to become a fearless speaker exhibiting stage might, not stage fright.

Here is the exercise, before you whisper each phrase, take a full bellyful of air and then pour all the air into that one phrase. Keep your throat open, and don't grind your vocal cords. Lift your whisper over your throat. Pause between phrases. Relax. Then take another full breath and whisper the next phrase. Whisper as if you were trying to reach the back of the room.

Once you've whispered the paragraph, go back to the start and speak conversationally. But again, pour all the air into each phrase and honour the silence between phrases. I can't stress that enough. Take your own sweet time at the forward slashes.

Also, take deep pleasure in enunciating each resonant vowel and delicious consonant. Give your lips and tongue the assignment of shaping every lovely syllable.

I like to do this exercise as though I were standing on second base in Yankee Stadium. I do it like an old-fashioned orator. I raise my arms to address the crowd, speak in a loud voice, and pretend. I spoon out each phrase very slowly because there are 60,000 people in the stands, and my voice has to travel a long way to reach their ears.

"The most precious things in speech are the... pauses."

— SIR RALPH RICHARDSON

Please, don't misunderstand me, I am not suggesting you deliver presentations pausing between each phrase. Instead, I am suggesting that you use this exercise as a tool to teach your mind and body how to slow the heck down.

Repetition is key. I bet that if you do this once a day for 21 straight days, you will cure yourself from speaking too fast. Let me know if it works.

7. Listen and study the body language of your audience

In today's world, listening is slowly becoming a lost art. Many speakers have sorely neglected this important part of verbal communication. A speaker understands that listening and studying the body language of his / her audience is an integral part of fearless public speaking. A speaker with listening skills picks up on body language and words not said by their audience. The speaker also gives the audience room to ask questions and clarify what they didn't hear.

Listening is an essential criterion for any engagement, whether a professional meeting or a social gathering. It impacts positively on the speaker's interaction with the audience. Speakers must listen to the body of their audience. To improve these listening skills, you will need to maintain good eye contact with the person you are communicating with and be present by giving them your full attention. Nod at the appropriate moments and make remarks, especially when it is time to answer any questions.

The art of listening is a desirable trait which speakers can utilise for the good of their speech. Listening also enables you to hear other speakers in your niche and

> *"To sway an audience, you must watch them as you speak."*
>
> — C. KENT WRIGHT

get useful tips on how to deliver a beautiful speech. Good listeners pick up information because they are silent and observant. They know when the crowd is bored. They know when a joke is not funny. Listening is essential in gaining trust.

When a speaker listens to his audience, he finds out if there is any sign of rebellion or boredom. With this intuition, a decision can be reached to either shorten the speech or change tactics.

Communication becomes more natural, and good camaraderie is established. An attentive listener solves most communication problems and ensures understanding. Attention should be paid to non-verbal cues, like gestures, voice tone, behaviour, and facial expressions.

Listening should not be over-emphasized as it remains one of the most important techniques for moving to stage might.

Chapter Exercise

List all you have learned from this chapter on converting your fear to might and compare it with your fright list compiled earlier. Also, record yourself on your phone as you give a speech. At first, do not apply any of the pointers provided in this chapter. Play it back and critically assess how good or bad the speech is, carefully noting the way your words flow. Record yourself a second time, but this time, apply all the techniques mentioned. Does the second recording sound better than the first? It is okay to place both recordings side-by-side and compare; let your ears be your guide.

CHAPTER FOUR

Preparing for The Stage

Chapter Outline

"It takes one hour of preparation for each minute of presentation time."

— WAYNE BURGRAFF

Preparation is one of the critical keys to a resounding success in anything we do. When you prepare for anything important, you largely eliminate your chances of failure. Yes, there may be some challenges at first, but if you keep at it with great effort, you will excel. This principle of practice uniquely applies to fearless public speaking.

"A speech is a solemn responsibility. The man who makes a bad 30 minutes speech to 200 people waste only half hour of his own time. But he wastes 100 hours of the audiences' time- more than four days- which should be a hanging offense."

— JENKIN LLOYD JONES

Stage fright and nervousness happen when people don't prepare before a speech. For some individuals, they forget what they are supposed to say and end up with a boring lecture. Other people rush through the process and fail to pass on the message of the speech to listeners. To conquer both issues, you must dedicate time to proper preparation. This chapter contains some of the most essential and practical strategies you can utilise for preparation. We will talk about how to develop self-confidence, practice persistently, know a lot about your subject, and conduct independent thinking.

To prepare well for your speech, you must do a lot of research online and offline while engaging in independent thinking. Knowledge of the subject is excellent, but what do you do with the knowledge gained? Some people get to know what the speech is about, but then they don't take things further. They don't create their own opinions or get to see how the subject affects the audience.

"Failure to prepare is preparing to fail."

— JOHN WOODEN

To prepare well, you must also learn how to strike a connection between what you will say and the impact it will have on your audience. The whole point of communicating is to be understood and to impart knowledge. You will feel nervous when you are not affecting or connecting with the audience.

Rehearsing your speech is a critical aspect of preparation.

This is an integral part of speaking. Rehearsing helps your role play as you envision how the speaking engagement will be. Prepare by rehearsing in front of the mirror, recording yourself, or even practising in the presence of friends.

If there is a time limit for your speech, preparation will help you get used to it and enable you to finish before your time. A significant reason you should practice with your friends as the audience is because it will help you feel at ease while facing a group of people. You will also learn how to make better eye contact and how to connect with an audience while speaking. In general, preparation through rehearsals puts you at ease, so you become less nervous and more familiar with the stage. Use your mobile device to record yourself, watch the recording, and constructively criticise your performance.

All these efforts will contribute to helping you fight off stage fright, overcome nervousness, and become a great speaker who gets better with every opportunity to speak to an audience. Nothing beats the importance of preparation in public speaking. Think of it as training you must embark upon to excel. For example, if a sprinter wants to break a world record, they have to practice. The only way the person can break a record is to prepare for the race before the day.

"Only the prepared speaker deserves to be confident."

— DALE CARNEGIE

Preparation helps you become familiar with all aspects of the speech so that when you stand before the audience, you will be bold. Confidence in your speech will come naturally, and you will be ready to convey your message eloquently and effortlessly.

Chapter Exercise

After reading this chapter, prepare yourself for a fictional speaking opportunity.

Preparing for Speaking

Planning for a speech begins in your mind!

- Reduce the double line to one below.

Your mind is a very crucial aspect of the planning stage because it is where you birth all your ideas, and it is also where confidence springs forth. You must begin with your mind, but how can you achieve this?

"*I believe that we learn by practice. Whether it means to learn to dance by practising dancing or to learn to live by practising living, the principles are the same. In each, it is the performance of a dedicated precise set of acts, physical or intellectual, from which comes shape of achievement, a sense of one's being, a satisfaction of spirit. One becomes, in some area, an athlete of God. Practice means to perform, over and over again in the face of all obstacles, some act of vision, of faith, of desire. Practice is a means of inviting the perfection desired.*"

— MARTHA GRAHAM

"Proper prior planning prevents pitiful poor performance."

— DON MEYER

Here are some of the importance of planning:

- Increases efficiency

- Gives direction

- Increases the chances of achieving the declared purpose

- Improves accountability

- Provides a measurement index of how much is being accomplished

- Increases foresight

- Provides clarity and keeps everything on track

- Improves morale

Chapter Exercise

The Five P's of Planning. Take each 'P' of planning and prepare for your next speaking opportunity.

"Before anything else, preparation is the key to success."

— ALEXANDER GRAHAM BELL

Five P's of Planning

1. Prepare the message

You need to have a specific message you intend to pass on to your audience. At this stage, don't be bothered about the introduction. Start by thinking about the central idea you want to share and hold an image of that idea in your mind. For example, if you're going to talk to your audience about the environment, you should know there are several aspects of the environment. It is better for you to talk about one or two aspects of the environment. For instance, you can speak about climate change as a topic and then hone in on that subject alone to build a clearer picture in the audiences' mind instead of diluting your topic by talking about the environment as a whole.

"If you don't know what you want to achieve in your presentation, your audience never will."

— HARVEY DIAMOND

Do not wander off into another part of your speech because doing this would spread you thin. Preparing the message entails knowing and understanding exactly what you want to achieve. This stage doesn't necessarily require research of any sort; what it does need is a mind that understands the direction it wants to go. No one can help you at this stage; watching videos or listening to speakers won't do it entirely. This is something you must find for yourself. Imagine for a moment that you either have an urgent situation at hand or a presentation at work that has pushed you towards picking up this book. Whatever the case may be, it is important that you have clarity of what you intend to achieve when you deliver a presentation, and that will assist your audiences to benefit from any presentation you deliver.

Now you don't have to think about your introduction to the idea of climate change, at this stage. Hold the image of climate change in your mind because it is the specific message you intend to convey. The next step is to properly develop the content around your topic which in this case is climate change.

2. Prepare the title of the speech/address

While the title helps you to shape your speech, it is the first part of the planning process because it is the foundation of the entire speech. It helps put things in perspective and focusses you to a theme. Without a title, you have nothing to talk about. The

"One important key to success is self-confidence. An important key to self-confidence is preparation."

—ARTHUR ASHE

moment you have your title, you should start planning your speech. The title should be interesting to your audience. For you to get the right title, you will need to spend quality time researching your topic. More importantly, if you have the option of choosing a topic yourself. Please settle for an idea you are passionate about as it would help in your delivery.

"The audience only pays attention as long as you know where you are going."

— PHILIP CROSBY

3. Prepare subtopics if any

Most topics can be extensive; hence, the reason subtopics are crucial.

You must know the EXACT area you will cover and tailor your speech on that basis. With specifics, you will speak confidently and with boldness without needless repetitions and loss of your thought process. While planning, always ask yourself, "What are the specifics of this speech?" and then find the answer through research.

4. Plan your speech in summaries

When done with specifics, move on to summarize them all into three major points. The keyword here is "major." There will be several other points that may be minor, but to keep your audience entertained and focused, focus on three MAJOR points. Ensure that you move gradually from one point to another, as planning ensures there is a smooth transition of your ideas. These three points will serve as the message of the speech the audience will remember. This also means preparing a strong middle part for your speech. Most times, we concentrate on the beginning and the end but forget that the middle is the bridge that links the two and, therefore, should be strong. The middle part of your speech should be written with the same flavour as the beginning and ending; it should not be an afterthought.

5. Plan the research

Next, you must brainstorm for ideas on the chosen topic. Traditionally, brainstorming is a method for generating ideas to solve a problem. It is usually carried out in a group situation under the direction of a facilitator. Now, the strength of brainstorming lies in the associations between ideas drawn by the participants; these participants are given free rein and are unconstrained by rules. This freethinking environment broadens the solution space and the gamut of solutions readily available once the session is completed.

In addition to the Five P's of Planning, if you work in Sales, as an Entrepreneur, Business Owner or a Professional, below is a deeper dive and a further explanation of the brainstorming technique that will enable you deliver any presentation excellently. The Brainstorming technique is a well-known one that allows any speaker to generate ideas in conjunction with others or members of a team, so whatever topic can be delivered to a very high standard.

Important information to consider when brainstorming

1. Begin with a targeted brief. Members of the brainstorming session should approach this sharply defined question, plan, or goal and stay on topic. Deviations should come as part of the plan if any.

2. Set a time limit. Depending on the problem's complexity, 15–60 minutes is normal. But going beyond that is also common practice; sometimes you must go slow when writing and planning.

3. Encourage weird ideas. Further to the ban on killer phrases, like "too expensive," keep the floodgates open so everyone feels free to blurt out thoughts as long as they're on topic.

4. Aim for quantity. Remember, quantity breeds quality; the sifting-and-sorting process comes later. Bring up ideas and record them without judging; there will be time for that much later.

5. Stay visual. Diagrams and Post-It notes help bring ideas to life and help others see things in different ways. Use these tools in helping you map out all your ideas and to keep your mind in check.

Unlike in the past, research is very flexible today. This realization is because of the availability of several sources of which the internet is prominent. With this in mind, let me share some brainstorming techniques with you, which will help you with flexibility and provide several options to try out. You can always hop from one technique to another; however, if you find a way to harness two – maybe three, then please go ahead.

Brainstorming Techniques

- **Mind Mapping**

Mind mapping is a visual tool for enhancing the brainstorming process. In essence, you're drawing a picture of the relationships among and between ideas.

Start by writing down your goal or challenge and ask participants to think of related issues. Layer by layer, add content to your map so you can visually see how. Mind mapping has become so popular, it's easy to find a mind mapping software online. The reality though, is that a large piece of paper and a few markers can also do the job.

- **Reverse Brainstorming**

Normally brainstorming asks participants to solve problems; that is how we know it to be. Reverse brainstorming is the complete opposite as it requires participants to come up with ways to **cause** a problem. You begin with a problem, then figure out how you would cause the same problems if it were up to you. Consider this a method that helps you find answers by working backwards to your goal. Apply this to your writing and presentation, then work backwards.

- **Gap Filling**

Begin with a statement of where you are, then write another about where you would like to be. At this stage, ask yourself how the gap from where you are to where you want to go can be filled. Collect all the ideas you generate from this session and follow up on the action steps you have written down. This can be applied to any situation. Going back to the issue around climate change, ask questions such as where do you want to be in resolving this problem? What do you want to see people do in addressing it? These questions put you in a *solution-search* mode, which is proactive.

- **Drivers Analysis**

Work with your group to discover the drivers behind the problem you're addressing. For example, in the Manufacturing industry, you ask, what's driving client loyalty down? What's driving the competition? What's driving a trend toward lower productivity? As you uncover the drivers, you begin to catch a glimpse of possible solutions.

- **The Five Whys**

Another tool that's often used in conjunction with brainstorming is the Five Whys. It can be an effective tool for getting the thought juices flowing. Start with a problem you're addressing and ask, "Why is this happening?" Once you have some answers, ask, "Why does this happen?" Continue the process five times – or more. Each time you ask a question, go deeper and explore every answer available. Getting down to the core of the problem is the goal.

- **Online Brainstorming (Brain-Netting)**

Perhaps not surprisingly, brain-netting involves brainstorming on the Internet. This requires someone to set up a system whereby individuals can share their ideas privately but then collaborate publicly. There are software companies that specialize in such types of systems, like Slack or Google Docs. Once ideas have been generated, it may be a good idea to come together in person.

- **Figure Storming**

Choose a figure from history or fiction with whom everyone is familiar—for example, Teddy Roosevelt or Mother Theresa. What would that individual do to manage the challenge or opportunity you're discussing? How might that figure's approach work well or poorly?

- **Step Ladder Brainstorming**

Start by sharing the brainstorming challenge with everyone in the room. Then send everyone, except two, out of the room to think about the challenge. Allow the two people in the room to come up with ideas for a short period and then allow one more person to enter the room. Ask the new person to share their ideas with the first two before discussing the ideas already generated. After a few minutes, ask another person to come in and then another. Eventually, everyone will be back in the room, and everyone will have shared his or her ideas with colleagues.

- **Rapid Ideation**

This simple technique can be surprisingly fruitful. Ask the individuals in your group to write down as many ideas as they can in a given period. Then either have them share the ideas aloud or collect responses. Often, you'll find certain ideas popping up repeatedly. Sometimes, these are the obvious ideas, but in other cases, they may provide revelations.

- **Charrette**

Imagine a brainstorming session in which 35 people from six departments are all struggling to come up with viable ideas. The process is time-consuming, boring, and—all too often—unfruitful. The charrette method breaks up the problem into smaller chunks with small groups discussing each element of the problem for a set period. Once each group has discussed one issue, their ideas are passed on to the next group, which builds on them. By the end of the charrette, each idea may have been discussed five or six times, and the ideas discussed have been refined.

- **What-If Brainstorming**

What-if brainstorming is typified by asking questions that don't stay within the realm of logic or reason. Almost anything is fair game. What is the advantage of these questions that have no logical barrier, you say? Well, they help take you out of your way; you are limited in thought when you ask about only the things you know. In what-if brainstorming, you can ask a question that maybe 100 years old or even create your own! What if aliens invade us? How would we cope and survive? What if plants take over the world? Will lettuce be kind enough to defend humanity? What if climate change is the love child of our planet's hatred? What can we do to change it? How would it be solved? What if Superman were facing this problem? How would he manage it? What if the problem were 50 times worse—or much less serious than it is? What would we do? These questions spur creativity and to get the juices flowing. It also lightens the mood and builds synergy in a team.

Research also helps you further streamline and narrow your topic as you discover more ideas. When you are done researching, you will have the points that will formulate the content of your speech, and this will also be your take-home message for the audience.

The above techniques will guide you on your way to planning, preparing and delivering a great speech. Planning entails a whole lot, and it is the bedrock on which an excellent presentation lies. If you succeed with the planning stage, you will deliver great content that will give you a flawless finish.

What we have done thus far is to give you a general idea of what planning entails so you know what you should be doing. Being prepared gets you on your way to becoming a fearless speaker. I have summarized below benefits of preparation. They are:

1. Self-Confidence

The first and best form of personal development you can give yourself is building self-esteem. Even if you are speaking about something exciting, if you don't portray confidence, you will lose the connection with the audience.

"*If you'd like to be good at something, the first thing to throw out the window is the notion of perfection.*"

— SCOTT BERKUN

Preparation gives you confidence; it helps you stand up tall and speak, knowing you are ready to pass on knowledge and information. To achieve this idea, you MUST believe in yourself and in your ability to deliver. Self-confident speakers also make mistakes, so avoid putting too much pressure on yourself because you want to be perfect. Forget about perfection and work on trusting your abilities and believing you can deliver your message excellently.

> *"The best way to conquer stage fright is to know what you are talking about."*
>
> — MICHAEL H. MESCON

When you build self-trust, it will translate into confidence, and you can share your ideas without fear. Cover all aspects and parts of the subject matter, so you walk on stage fully prepared.

2. Enhanced knowledge in the subject matter

Speaking about an idea or a topic indicates that you have some knowledge in that area. But most times, people fail to gain an understanding because they assume that the basic idea is enough.

Speaking to your friends and family about something differs from speaking to a group of people. If you want to be confident, you must go the extra mile by getting additional knowledge and knowing everything about what you will talk about. Read books about the topic, research online, listen to podcasts, and be mentally prepared for the speech. When you are knowledgeable in your subject area, you can answer any question. You will also speak with certainty as well because you've got the facts and figures to prove your assertions.

3 Increased Credibility

When you speak, your audience knows immediately your worth which can only be achieved when a speaker has adequately prepared.

Master the art of being prepared for any speech or presentation and conquer the fear of Public Speaking.

CHAPTER FIVE

On Stage

Chapter Outline

"During the first few minutes of your presentation, your job is to assure the audience that you are not going to waste their time and attention."

— DALE LUDWIG AND GREG OWEN-BOGER

Every speech has three segments, no matter how you slice it. Understanding this basic structure will save you a lot of headaches in planning and delivering your speech. This understanding can also assist you in the delivery of all types of speeches, including impromptu speeches. Yes, it may take practice, but it is doable.

The three segments that constitute a great speech are **opening**, **middle**, and **conclusion**. These segments sometimes go by different titles, but their function remains the same. There are cases where more sub-segments will be added to individual speeches, and approached with the three segments in mind. From here on, I will break down every section and show the importance of each to the overall speech. Every step in this is essential and should be treated as such. A weak ending will water down the effect created by a strong opener and middle and vice-versa.

Opening

On entering the stage

The moment you've been introduced, and the stage is given to you, take about 4-5 seconds to do the breathing exercise mentioned earlier. Taking control of your nerves can never be over-estimated. You can look around at your audience while doing this if you don't want to feel awkward when doing the exercise. The breathing exercise should relax your nerves and drive away overwhelming anxiety that comes with being in the public eye. Remember that the speakers you look up to do something similar whenever they face overwhelming situations, so there is no need to feel like a hack. Take deep breaths and push them out while smiling and looking around.

How to begin your speech

There are several ways to start your speech, and any combination you choose is up to you and the situation at hand. Knowing a lot of ways to kick off a speech can be good and bad at the same time. Why? Knowing a bunch of these opening techniques doesn't automatically grant you proficiency; this comes from experience and practice. But to give you a variety, I will mention a few and let you decide which one you want to start with.

Before words leave your mouth, check your body language. Is your posture strong? What about your stage presence? Remember, this is a fancy way of asking if you are confident, and this would be the case if you took the time to write and practice your speech properly.

Four ways to open your speech

"During the first few minutes of your presentation, your job is to assure the audience members that you are not going to waste their time and attention."

— DALE LUDWIG AND GREG OWEN-BOGER

A good speaker worries about his presentation while a great speaker is concerned about not wasting the time of his audience. The two may seem the same, but they are not. One is concerned with himself; the other is obsessed with giving value. I want you to be a great speaker. I want you to be the speaker who is obsessed with delivering value to the audience out in front. So, what does a great speaker do when they are in front of an audience?

"There are three things to aim at in public speaking: first, to get into your subject, then to get your subject into yourself, and lastly, to get your subject into the heart of your audience."

— ALEXANDER GREGG.

1. Compliment the audience and organiser

Everyone likes compliments. Compliments show that someone took special notice of you and put in an effort to communicate this to you. Compliments show you are graceful and considerate in speech and attitude. You immediately bring the audience over to your side when you compliment them and mean it. Express how honoured and happy you are to be in front of them and how much you look forward to sharing what you have with them. The culture of honour and respect is a valuable custom to maintain.

"The heart and soul of good writing is research; you should write not what you know but what you can find out about".

— ROBERT J. SAWYER

"I love the early process of asking questions about a story and deciding which questions matter most."

— DIANE SAWYER

2. Start with a story

Everyone loves a good story. You can tell a story from your own life or from something you heard. Whatever the case may be, you should be entertaining. Don't be a stiff, boring speaker that drowns the room in the gloom. Tell stories that loosen the atmosphere and bring the audience's attention to you. Stories are lovely icebreakers.

3. Ask a question

Openers are best when they pull in engagement from the audience. You can pose a problem to the audience and ask for an answer. Take your time when doing this and milk the situation for all its worth – without wasting time, of course. The point of asking a question(s) from the beginning is to capture the audience's attention. Questions facilitate camaraderie and build a sense of community; they give the feeling you all are in search of one answer.

4. Quote research

Quoting straight from study and citing your source or sources is a secure way to start as it lends credibility to everything you will say afterwards and paints you as someone in the *know*. You can begin by making your first statement a shocker; this is especially effective with sensitive issues that tend to be overlooked. Drop the shocking comment followed by the research to back it up, then allow your words to sink in.

4 Ways not to start your speech

- Apologising

Don't start your speech with an apology. It doesn't matter what you are apologising for. Don't do it. It demeans and waters down anything else you will say afterwards.

- Inappropriate jokes

Don't be the guy that is loud and uncouth. Inappropriate jokes aren't a good idea when opening or during your speech.

- A long-winded opening

Go straight to the point. There is no need to say anything that doesn't push your speech forward or is pertinent to the matter at hand. Refuse distracting commentaries and its ilk.

- Admitting to not planning

You may feel like this is you being honest, and the audience will understand, but I assure you they will not. Don't even think about talking about your lack of preparation; you must avoid this move like a plague.

Middle of the Speech

"If you have an important point to make, don't try to be subtle or clever. Use a pile driver. Hit the point once. Then come back and hit it again. Then hit it a third time-a tremendous whack."

— WINSTON S. CHURCHILL

By the middle of your speech, there is a high probability that your audience will lose interest.

Research shows that attention span is highest at the beginning of a speech and significantly reduces by the middle of the speech only to go back up towards the end. The reason the audience suddenly regains interest is that they have a sense you are drawing your speech to a close!

"Good transitions can make a speech more important to the audience because they feel they are being taken to a positive conclusion without having to travel a bumpy road."

— JOE GRIFFITH

The middle of your speech is the body and, as is expected, contains the bulk of the information you want to communicate. From your opening and later statements, the audience has been introduced to the subject and your raison d'être. You need only to keep your descriptions clear, and illustrations concise, and your message should flow as you had planned. Don't overwhelm your audience with too many points. It is much more valuable to make a few points well than to have too many points, which aren't made satisfactorily.

Here are some points to help you reel back your audience if you notice their interest is waning. Do this every time you present a speech because it helps.

a. Question & Answers

Plan your speech so the middle part will gradually wind down into a Q&A segment. It need not be this big thing; you can make it look like a recap of all you have already said. Q&As are the perfect way to test your audience retention capacity while engaging them and pushing away any lack of interest that may have set in.

b. Change your visual aid

If you were using flow charts before your audience's attention trickled away from your direction, then switch it up. Try illustrations, audio, video, or any other format that carries similar information. You must plan for this. Spicing things up is an excellent way to reset the atmosphere and bring everyone back into the flow.

c. Tell a story

Stories work as a beautiful transition tool when interests are waning. Inputting a story has to seem a natural progression rather than a forced element. Plan with relevant stories in mind for days when your audience are extra distracted. Think up stories on the spot also or improvise! You can always call up someone from the audience and ask them to participate in your story or to help demonstrate what you are saying.

Conclusion

This is when you complete your presentation. More discussions on concluding a speech will be covered in more detail in Chapter 7. The reader is reminded to ensure their conclusion is as good as their opening and the middle. This can only happen when it is planned in advance. I have seen experienced speakers fall flat when they conclude their speech. It should never be abrupt or lacking in depth. It is pertinent to note that the conclusion if good is likely to be the take home message for your audience and that is the reason why you need to make it brilliant.

CHAPTER SIX

The Perfect Poise: How to Remain Unshaken Amidst the Flashlights

Chapter Outline

Your delivery

"Oratory is the power to talk people out of their sober and natural opinions."

— JOSEPH CHATFIELD

You don't get a second chance to make a first impression. Having a commanding presence when making a delivery is everything, whether it is on a stage or not. Presence is vital for several reasons but, more importantly, because it aids flawless delivery. The public speakers, who are consistent with speaking and improving their craft, never suffer from low self-esteem because they feel comfortable in front of an audience, and they can deliver with style and perfect poise.

"The energy level of the audience is the same as the speakers. For better...or for worse."

— ANDRAS BANETH

It takes about 4 minutes to create an impression on a person, and in those 4 minutes, 90% of the idea is formed within the first 90 seconds. This means that if you want to have an excellent delivery, you must get the attention of your audience and make an excellent first impression. A good first impression is a key to getting your audience's rapt attention.

The ideas you will discover in this chapter will help you speak with style and poise so you can deliver excellently. Remember, first impressions matter, so have this in mind as you read.

"The way you overcome shyness is to become so wrapped up in something that you forget to be afraid."

— LADY BIRD JOHNSON

Planning your Poise

- **Immediately connect with your audience**

"You can speak well if your tongue can deliver the message of your heart."

— JOHN FORD

"Be yourself; everyone else is already taken," was famously said by Oscar Wilde. The way you connect with your audience matters a lot, and it is something you must do immediately once you start speaking. Now there are some little things you must do while speaking that will help you connect with the audience. They are:

a. **Vocal Variety** - Vocal variety makes a speech fascinating; don't use a flat tone from the beginning to the end. Raise your mood when you want to emphasise a point and bring it down when you want them to introduce a new idea. To become perfect with the vocal variety, you must practice intentionally.

b. **Maintain eye contact** - Maintain eye contact while speaking and be bold enough to look directly at your audience instead of over their heads. The goal is to connect with the audience, and you can achieve this when you speak and maintain eye contact with them.

c. **Use Pause** - Taking pauses during a speech has a way of giving you power. You can talk rapidly and may seem smart in some circles, but most often than not, people will perceive you as nervous. Being deliberately slow and nuanced is an asset to any speaker that aspires to be great. Pausing provides a moment of silence to calm incessant talking, allows time for your brain to catch up with your mouth, provides your listener with space to process your message, and highlights important points, thereby granting potency to your message.

d. **Keep it short and never apologise for your shortcomings** - While speaking, there might be some shortcomings on your part. This is a common issue while speaking, but you shouldn't apologise for it. Maintain a focused approach to your speech and continue to hold the attention of the audience. No one ever complained about a short speech.

e. **Speak in a conversational tone** - Don't speak to the audience as though they are robots. You are talking to real people, and it helps if you use a conversational tone. Remember that you are sharing an idea with them or convincing them of something, so speak as though you are talking to a friend.

f. **Don't imitate, be authentic** - In ensuring excellent delivery, we are often tempted to talk like someone else because we believe in their style of delivery. But this is a wrong move; you must always remember to be yourself through the entire speech process. When you are 100% authentic, the audience will enjoy connecting with you, and this will serve as an opportunity for you to speak excellently.

g. **Concentrate on your message** - In order for you to deliver an amazing presentation you will need to fully concentrate on your message instead of focusing on yourself. When you concentrate on your message, you remove the pressure on yourself by channelling all your focus on your audience instead of yourself. Due to this change in approach you will find it easier to engage with your audience because you'll become available to them and your presence is felt.

"Speech is power: speech is to persuade, to convert, to compel."

— RALPH WALDO EMERSON

The best way to connect with any audience is to share the 4 Fs which entail:

- Flaws

- Failures

- Frustrations

- First

Audiences will connect easily with speakers when they sense that the speaker is just like them. If you are speaking about something new that you want the audience to do, they must know if they can trust you. The best way to show trust is by being honest about your journey with the idea by using these 4 Fs. First, you share some of your flaws, which are a testament to how you had to overcome the challenges.

Then you express some of your failures, which will help the audience know that it is okay to have faults. At this stage, you will gain the trust of the audience and strike a genuine connection with them. Share some of your frustrations and your first-time leaping. These will enable you to strengthen the relationship with the audience, which will be crucial for effective delivery while speaking.

"Pay less attention to what men say. Just watch what they do."

— DALE CARNEGIE

Know Your Audience Profile

You will always need to adapt your communication style to your audience so it matches how they think because if you don't, you will certainly lose your audience.

There are three types of profiles you must consider when giving speeches:

a. The Visual pattern

The people in this category connect easily when you show them images that aid visualization for them. In speaking with this group, you must strike a balance between what you say and what you show them. These people are the personification of the term, show and tell. The typical visual learner prefers to read the information in a textbook or on a whiteboard rather than listen to a lecture. Visualization techniques help them remember things. They often enjoy doodling and drawing and can use this practice as a study tool. Visual learners use sight words in their everyday terminology.

For example, they might say, *Let's look at this.* They easily remember details, including colours and spatial arrangements, and they excel at memory games that require a visual recall. They often have a good sense of direction because they can visualise maps and directions in their mind. Visual learners learn best when they can see the material being taught. They follow instructions better when they can see a demonstration first rather than being told how to do something. Use images, maps, graphs, and other visual representations when presenting to this group.

b. The Auditory profile

This kind of pattern consists of people who love to listen and can even enjoy speeches that may be termed "boring." The auditory learners will want to know more about what you are saying, and if you speak right, you can get their attention. Auditory learners need to listen, speak, and interact with learning. They are often social butterflies. Help the auditory learners in your session/group with these techniques. During sessions, ask auditory learners to repeat ideas in their own words. Record your speech so auditory learners can listen to them more than once. Allow any struggling auditory learner to take an oral exam instead of a written one. Create activities/exercises that include a social element, such as paired readings, group work, experiments, projects, and performances. Modulate your vocal tone, inflection, and body language during lectures. Call on auditory learners to answer questions. Lead discussions and reward participation.

c. The Kinaesthetic profile

The kinaesthetic learner loves physical activity, which makes the listening experience exciting for him/her. Kinaesthetic learners typically learn best by doing. They are naturally good at physical activities, like sports and dance. They enjoy learning through hands-on methods. They usually like how-to guides and action-adventure stories. They might pace while on the phone or take breaks from studying to get up and move around. Some may seem fidgety, having a hard time sitting still in class. Kinaesthetic learners learn best through doing, including manipulating items, simulations, role-plays, and other methods for presenting subject matter that physically involve them in the learning process. They enjoy and learn well from experimenting and first-hand experience. Further, they learn best when activities are varied during a session.

Be aware that you will have a mix of these profiles in your audience, so you must tailor your speech to capture all their attention. Your words should paint pictures, and your personal experiences should affect their feelings. Also, try to connect with your audience using meaningful stories that add value to their experience. It might be a little challenging for you to bring together all these profiles and talk to them, so it carries everyone along, but the fruit is worth every ounce of effort.

Communication skills are not the easiest of skills to master. To make matters worse, they may not come naturally to most. So, having diverse learners in a session or as an audience can be a bit much for most people, but it need not be this way. Remembering some key concepts will prepare you towards success as you write down your presentation and eventually deliver the said presentation. Writing with these profiles in mind doesn't always have to be tedious if you follow the advice I lay down and are open to communicating and adjusting what you already work with.

You should know that 42% of what you say is mostly forgotten within the first 20 minutes of hearing it. More so, within half a day of the speech, your audience will not recall the remaining 58% even if your statement was well-prepared. Most of what is said will be forgotten, but you can still make an effort to connect with the audience so you can build experience. This can be discouraging when you consider how long you have to speak to try and convey a message but working with this knowledge will better place you in a position of success. There are other tools to engage the audience besides your voice and gesticulations. Mastering those tools is part of your calling as a speaker.

Try as much as you can to engage with their emotions and if you succeed in doing that, they are likely to recall your speech better. Generally, your audience would remember:

- Information in visual form
- Repeated information

- Introductions and conclusions
- Information that is repeated
- Information that is different

In terms of the percentage of what people recall:

- 12% - What they Read
- 18% - What they Hear
- 30% - What they Observe
- 52% - What they Read, Hear and Observe
- 70% - What they Read, Hear, Observe and Informed of
- 92% - What they Read, Hear, Observe, Informed and Experience.

This is the reason experiential learning is the key if you are a coach and you want your students to retain most of the information they are taught. Experiential learning also known as EXL is a process when you learn through experience or by doing.

Chapter Exercise

The most exciting fact about this chapter is that you can use the concepts shared immediately and get results. You can create a great first impression every time you speak, but first, you must practice fervently with every speaking opportunity that comes your way by attempting to utilise all the profiles discussed above. If you want to be a great speaker you will need to engage all the profiles and make sure that you design your speech or training to enable maximum recollection by your audience.

If Everything Fails, Use the Power of Positive Words

Speaking words of affirmation into the life of your audience goes a long way. In today's world, there is a lot of toxicity, bitterness, and negativity so much so people unconsciously flinch when hurtful words are hurled at them. The world has produced hardened humans due to individual environments, upbringing, societal expectations, and influence. The level of negativity is so high that when a person receives compliments or positive words of affirmation, it is either received with scepticism or warmth, which can affect their whole day. Before you begin your speech, pay compliments to a few people in the audience. It works most of the time and makes them receptive to your message.

"Words have incredible power. They can make people's hearts soar, or they can make people's hearts sore."

— DR. MARDY GROTHE

Positive words are like water; they flow, soothe, and refresh all those who come in contact with it. Positive energy is infectious. The more you use this on your audience, the more they warm up to you.

"Once you get people laughing, they're listening, and you can tell them almost anything."

— HERBERT GARDNER

A person who may want to interrupt your speech may be stopped with a kind word. Think of the speaker who compliments his audience and is interested in their well-being by speaking positive words before they begin the speech.

Positive words breed positive energy that spreads like an aura from the giver to the recipients around. Sadly, positivity is lacking in many lives, families, and workplaces and, as a result, in many communities. We need to say positive words to people irrespective of their background and stage in life. Positive words are like rays of sunshine that make everyone feel better, and with this atmosphere, you get the calm and poise needed to make an excellent delivery.

"Successful leaders see the opportunities in every difficulty rather than the difficulty in every opportunity."

— REED MARKHAM

You can make a person's day by being your cheerful self or by drawing him or her away from the negativity that has surrounded him or her. Just because you never know who needs it in your audience, do your best to maintain a positive outlook on life and things. See the good in people and even in adverse circumstances, be open enough to see the bright side of things. Indeed, there is always someone who needs a positive word or two. Spread warmth, joy, and peace through your words and your warm smile. Positivity is what we all need. It doesn't matter if it is a kind word or a genuine compliment; do not forget to spread positivity around before or during a speech.

Planning for Rejection When Everything Else Fails

What happens when your speech doesn't resonate with your audience? Many public speaking books do not make provisions for this, but you must be prepared to take it all in your stride.

I remember my early days of public speaking. I didn't know all that I know now. I wasn't fearless, and I did not have the keys I am putting in this book. It took a lot of nervous mistakes and rejections before I became as good as I am today. Had someone told me to brace myself, perhaps it wouldn't have hurt as much.

It hurts to be rejected, especially when you think you have delivered a good speech, and it didn't quite turn out the way you expected. As we make our way through life, there is bound to be unpleasant memories and rejection in our careers.

Rejection hurts, especially if it is unexpected. It makes you lose confidence, and it induces low self-esteem. These sad feelings have made many people live in fear of rejection, making them afraid to chase their dreams of being renowned speakers. Many people struggle with doubt and need guidance on what to do in these situations.

"Always give a speech that you would like to hear."

— Andrii Sedniev

Overcoming the anxiety that comes with rejection is possible. If you are experiencing this on stage or in public gatherings, here are some ways to make sure you are not engulfed with fear:

- **Be at your best**

Giving your best minimises your chances of failure and, therefore, the fear of rejection or being booed after your speech. For any task, you set your mind to, put in your best. Although some results are unpredictable, you minimise the chances of being rejected if you are good at what you do.

- **Believe in yourself**

Do not see yourself as undeserving of an applause or standing ovation. If you are unhappy with your body type or how you look in a suit or dress, do something about it but never let rejection affect your confidence. Everyone is unique in their own way. If you are so afraid to give things a try because of how you look or people's reactions, you will go nowhere. Do not set yourself up for rejection. If you do, you make yourself an easy target by attracting that which you most fear.

- **Be positive**

When you speak positive things in your life, you attract positivity to yourself. It is called the law of visualisation and manifestation. Use your imagination to create the perfect situation for yourself and pre-empt all scenarios and how you would react to them. Be clear about what you want people to react to after your speech.

Focus on situations or topics that only make you feel confident. Do not be distracted by hurtful words and incidents until you achieve them. Do away with toxic environments, friendships, relationships, and situations and embrace positivity.

- **Face your fears head-on**

"Great things happen to those who don't stop believing, trying, learning, and being grateful."

— ROY T. BENNETT

When you confront your fears, you discover that they are only shadows. These limiting factors stop you from aspiring higher and seeing the bigger picture. Some situations happen for the greater good. Once you entertain this notion, you will take things in your stride and overcome the fear of rejection.

- **Life goes on**

Irrespective of whatever happens, see it as a phase in your life. If I had stopped speaking after my first rejection, I wouldn't be where I am today. In a couple of days or weeks, you will get over it, and life will go on. If you have this mentality of always getting back up after being rejected, you will shrug it off when rejection comes. The fear of rejection shouldn't stop you from booking another event to speak at or from delivering the next presentation or from sharing your thoughts amongst friends or colleagues. Don't spend all your time wondering what could have been. Learn to develop a thick skin and brace yourself beforehand.

"*Be yourself; everyone else is already taken.*"

— OSCAR WILDE

- **The best of us get rejected**

The best speakers have been laughed at. They have been rejected at some point! Rejection is a phase everyone goes through. Sometimes being rejected has nothing to do with you but the person at the other end. Do not carry the extra burden of other people's actions. You have a right to react to each scenario the way you want to. You are not responsible for their actions. That's on them, not on you. Rejection doesn't mean you are unworthy of a particular stage or audience. When you know your self-worth, you will not let these words have any power over you.

- **Let go of being a victim**

"A rejection is nothing more than a necessary step in the pursuit of success"

— ROBERT FOSTER BENNETT

Instead of being frightened all the time and using it as an excuse not to land the next speaking gig or to deliver the next key presentation, let go of the victim mentality. Bad things that are destined to happen will happen despite how careful you are. When you see yourself as a victim, you attract negative energy and remain in a position without moving forward. That's a lose-lose situation. What's the worst that can happen? Don't be carried away with past rejections. Learn to leave things that belong to the past in the past.

- **Be resilient**

Those with a can-do spirit do not stay down for too long. All endeavours have their ups and downs, and it is expected that people ride the storm. Life is uncertain, and all we can do is hang on for the ride. Having a resilient mindset makes you prepared for eventualities in the public speaking industry. Lack of self-confidence can stop you from seeing what an amazing person you are and under utilising your potential. It can stop you from working on your insecurities and reaching for dreams that can bring you happiness.

Don't let your fear of rejection be hinged on activities that may or may not happen. One moment in your life doesn't define your speaking career. If you are rejected, look for other opportunities and move on. If you are a business owner, a professional or

"Do not judge me by my success, judge me by how many times I fell down and got back up again."

— NELSON MANDELA

an entrepreneur, go back and practice more and get better at the art of speaking. If you hold back from speaking, you miss a chance at other opportunities. You might wake up one day to discover that life has passed you by while you mope and worry about things that will not matter in a year or two.

"There are always three speeches, for every one you actually gave. The one you practiced, the one you gave, and the one you wish you gave."

— DALE CARNEGIE

Trust your journey. Personal growth comes to those who cultivate inner strength and peace. It takes courage and confidence. Don't give people so much power over your emotional state and be gentle on yourself. As you become less afraid, you become less intimated by rejection.

CHAPTER SEVEN

Conclude Like A Champ!

Chapter Outline

Conclusion

"Be not afraid of life. Believe that life is worth living, and your belief will help create the fact."

— WILLIAM JAMES

As you conclude your speech, end on a high note. If you talked about a depressing topic or something sensitive, shed hope as you round up. Be deliberate about encouraging and motivating your audience to act.

List out areas you believe they would benefit immensely if they only put it into practice. It is always a good point to summarise your whole speech at the end and hone in on the essence of the whole presentation. A strong conclusion smooths out any bumpy encounter you may have had during a speech, right from the opening to the conclusion.

Conclusions shouldn't be abrupt or lacking in finesse; take your time to craft them to perfection. Once more, here are the things to do on stage as you conclude:

- Summarise your main points

- End on a high note

- List your call-to-action

- Encourage

What do you want the audience to gain from your speech? Let your take home message be clear by the time you get to the end of your speech or presentation. You must ensure you conclude like a champ. We must finish strong by also considering the concluding part of your speech. Most people erroneously focus on the body of the speech itself and do not prepare for the conclusion. The end is just as important as the introduction and every other part of the speech. Sometimes, the audience may forget what you said mid-way into the speech, but they will always remember how you ended it.

The conclusion is not an opportunity for you to rush off the main points or walk off the stage. The end is an opportunity for you to strike a great connection with your audience and pass on a powerful message as you finish your speech. In this chapter, you will discover some of the most effective ways through which you can conclude your speech most powerfully.

"If you can't write your message in a sentence, you can't say it in an hour."

— Diana Booher

Generally, your conclusion is a summary of everything you presented in the body of the speech, but there is a way to go about it. The review must be structured in three short parts, which we will discuss below.

1. Inform the audience what you've told them before

To become a great speaker, you must learn how to conclude by informing the audience what you've already told them earlier on in the speech.

"Ask yourself, 'If I had only sixty seconds on the stage, what would I absolutely have to say to get my message across."

— Jeff Dewar

You mustn't move around in circles, speaking vaguely and irrelevantly. Go straight to the point, and keep it simple. The audience, at this point, knows that you are about to conclude and isn't expecting a "body" of conclusion, which could be lengthy. So, while preparing to speak, you need to ask this critical question, "What do I want to say to the audience?" When you get an answer to the question, please go right ahead and say it. If, while speaking, you recall some major points not mentioned in the body of the speech, do not raise this point because you'll confuse the audience.

2. Conclude with a definite tone

After identifying what you want to say, you will need to conclude with a definite tone. Some people rush through the process because they think it is insignificant, but if you do this, you will lose the connection with the audience. Conclude with a definite tone that isn't too high or too low. Let your conclusion flow from one point to another so the audience gets the main idea of what you are saying.

If you use presentation slides, try not to read through them word for word. Pick out the main points without excessively elaborating on them and make sure you get the attention of the audience from the start of the conclusion to the end. Sometimes, you may have enough time for your speech so that after your conclusion, you can have time for a Question & Answer (Q&A) session. Now having a Q&A session doesn't apply to All public speaking opportunities, so you must know if yours should include this. A Q&A session can help take the pressure off you for a few seconds while someone asks a question, and you give a reply. With or without a Q&A session, if you practice and know what you need to say, you will deliver an excellent conclusion.

3. Summarising what you have said

Know how to summarize what you want to say. The body of your speech is a general idea, but the conclusion presents the main points.

These main points must be summarised in the most concise way possible. For example, if you talked about a problem and then proffered solutions to the issue, you need to focus on both. The summary of your speech should be on what the problem is (directly) and then list the solution you mentioned. Your summaries can be simple sentences that the audience understands without having to overthink or rationalise. At this point, don't try to "prove" anything or convince them. You have already done most of the main work in the body of your speech, so keep your summaries short, simple, and impactful. Use more action verbs if you are inspiring them to take action. But if it is an inspirational speech, you should use more compelling words. Ensure you summarise what you've said and give the audience something to think about the speech.

"Think like a wise man but communicate in the language of the people."

— WILLIAM BUTLER YEATS

If you prepared adequately for your speech, the concluding section won't be problematic for you. Some people struggle with the conclusion because they don't practice enough, so they are not familiar with what they are supposed to say at the end.

The importance of preparation is one reason why we discussed it extensively in Chapter Four. You can avoid mistakes and issues through constant training before the big day.

The concluding part of every public speaking event should be delivered confidently. Think about it as you would the end of an opera. In a musical performance, the last musical notes give the song a brilliant finish. More so, if you didn't start well at the beginning of your speech, you can make up for it in the conclusion. Use the steps above to execute the PERFECT finish. Do it repeatedly, and as you do, you'll become better.

Fearless Speaking System

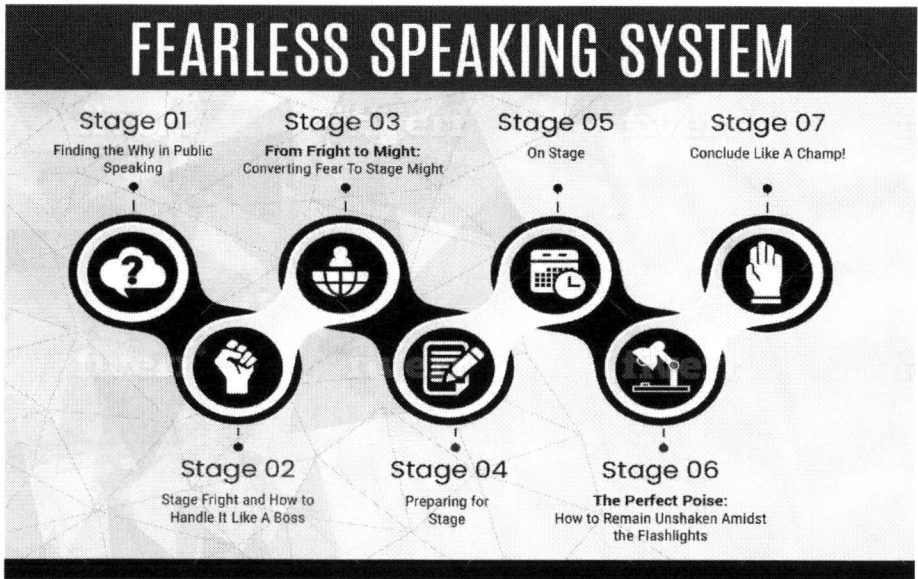

YOUR TIME TO ACT!

"Do not go where the path may lead, go instead where there is no path and leave a trail."v

— RALPH WALDO EMERSON

It is now time to jump and grow your wings on your way down. Taking action means you will overcome your fear of speaking in public and become an eloquent speaker.

When we started this journey, I shared a personal account of my struggles with public speaking and how I gradually overcame such fears. Well, my most significant asset, which enabled me to become even more confident, was my desire to get better.

As we finish with this concluding section, you must know that to succeed with this idea, you must keep the goal in front of you. You must be desirous of it because this is a journey of self-realisation.

"The difference between a successful person and others is not a lack of strength not a lack of knowledge but rather a lack of will."

— VINCE LOMBARDI

You have just discovered and read amazing strategies that will work for you, but the question is, what's next? What will you do with all you've learned? If you genuinely want to overcome your fear of public speaking, then you will implement all you've learned immediately.

Go back through the chapters and execute the ideas gained because you are convinced of its capacity to transform your speaking ability. Honestly, there is no magic wand you can wave that can suddenly make you feel confident. Nothing can replace the importance of consistent practice.

"A book may give you excellent suggestions on how best to conduct yourself in the water, but sooner or later you must get wet, perhaps even strangle and be "half scared to death." There are a great many "wet less" bathing suits worn at the seashore, but no one ever learns to swim in them. To plunge is the only way."

— DALE CARNEGIE

You must put yourself in situations that make you feel uncomfortable and try to overcome them. Think of your fears as a box you are in that is very comfortable, but in that comfort zone, you are depriving yourself of growth.

The desire to help people prompted me to establish the Essex Public Speaking Academy. The academy enables students, professionals, and business own-

> *"The world is waiting for your words."*
>
> — ARVEE ROBINSON

ers in the United Kingdom to practice and develop their craft in a safe place before thrusting themselves into the limelight.

The Essex Public Speaking Academy helps people see themselves differently after acquiring the important skills of speaking fearlessly. With the training they receive from us, they can go into the world and become the very best speakers, because they have mastered the art of speaking confidently and eloquently in public. Some of our clients have become better at their careers leading to advancement on the corporate ladder, while others who are engaged in business ventures have turned leads to more sales and increased profits for their companies. Others have become excellent Public Speakers drawing large audiences to their event, training or program. This can also be YOU.

Don't worry if you don't have an opportunity to attend the Essex Public Speaking Academy personally as we have other means through which you can attend our online programs (webinars, live video meetings, Facebook lives etc).

"You gain strength, courage and confidence by every experience in which you really stop to look fear in the face. You are able to say to yourself, 'I have lived through this horror. I can take the next thing that comes along.' You must do the thing you think you cannot do."

— ELEANOR ROOSEVELT

"Buried deep within each of us is a spark of greatness, a spark than can be fanned into flames of passion and achievement. That spark is not outside of you; it is born deep within you."

— James A. Ray

Some of our clients have become better at their careers leading to advancement on the corporate ladder, while others who are engaged in business ventures have turned leads to more sales and increased profits for their companies. Others have become excellent Public Speakers drawing large audiences to their event, training or program. This can also be YOU. Don't worry if you don't have an opportunity to attend the Essex Public Speaking Academy personally as we have other means through which you can attend our online programs (webinars, live video meetings, Facebook lives etc).

I will like you to remember these three key elements. They are DESIRE, STRATEGY, and a reliable SUPPORT SYSTEM, such as the Essex Public Speaking Academy. The three elements are vital for success in public speaking. You've got to develop the personal desire, combine it with the strategies in this book, and get help through coaching. This is how you can sustain your growth in becoming a fearless public

"There is freedom in stepping out and taking risks when you know at any given moment, you can always begin again."

— EVA GREGORY

speaker. Life is akin to attending school and learning; you are now at the level where you need to gain expertise in public speaking. At this phase, you have received all you need to get started.

Remember that it isn't about what you know; it is all about what you DO with what you know. Knowledge of public speaking *without* execution doesn't help. As you put this book down, start practising. John Ford said you could speak well if your tongue can deliver the message of your heart.

You will overcome your fear of public speaking, and you will be empowered enough to make a difference and help someone else.

I'll leave you with the words of DH Lawrence, "Be still when you have nothing to say; when genuine passion moves you, say what you have got to say and say it hot!"

Cheers to your speaking success!

Printed in Poland
by Amazon Fulfillment
Poland Sp. z o.o., Wrocław

57952986R00115

Top 25 Secrets of Golf
Copyright © 2004, 2005 by Mike L. Mc Colgan
2253 Deer Oak Way, Suite 252
Danville, Ca. 94506

ISBN 0-9666893-2-1

Second Edition

Published by MLM Books
2253 Deer Oak Way, Suite 252
Danville, Ca. 94506

To order: send $15.95 + $1.00 s/h ($16.95)
to the above address payable to MLM Books
or call toll free 1-877-LUV-GOLF
1-877-588-4653
Also available at www.amazon.com

PRINTED IN THE UNITED STATES OF AMERICA

TOP 25 SECRETS OF GOLF

OF GOLF

BY

MIKE L. MC COLGAN

Second Edition

Introduction

Golf is 95% mental and 5% mental. In this book I am going to reveal the top 25 Secrets of Golf that will help you improve your game and increase your enjoyment of the great game of golf. Whether you are young, old, new, bad, good, or a great golfer, these secrets will help you become a better golfer. These top 25 secrets have been compiled over the last 40 years of playing, writing and working in the game of golf. I am a single digit handicapper who has played great golf courses all over the world, inventor of the Macasonic (ultrasonic grip and golf club cleaner), author of two successful golf books—*101 Sins of Golf* and *101 Superstitions of Golf*—editor of *Golf Today Magazine,* and partner and father of MJ Mc COLGAN, 4-time California Special Olympics Golf Gold Medal Champion (2001, 2002, 2003 and 2004), 2-time National Silver Medal Champion (2002, 2003), and 2004 National Gold Medal Champion in the alternate shot Ryder Cup format. Enjoy this book and Hit Em Straight!

Acknowledgements

I acknowledge and thank my wife Linda, son Michael J. and the 9000 Special Olympic Golfers who inspired me to write this book.

NUMBER 25

DON'T BE SO HARD ON YOURSELF

Only 10% of golfers shoot 90 or better. Enjoy the game, the beautiful surroundings, and the people. You probably will not be playing on the professional golf tours. Don't be so hard on yourself and you will enjoy the game more and shoot lower scores.

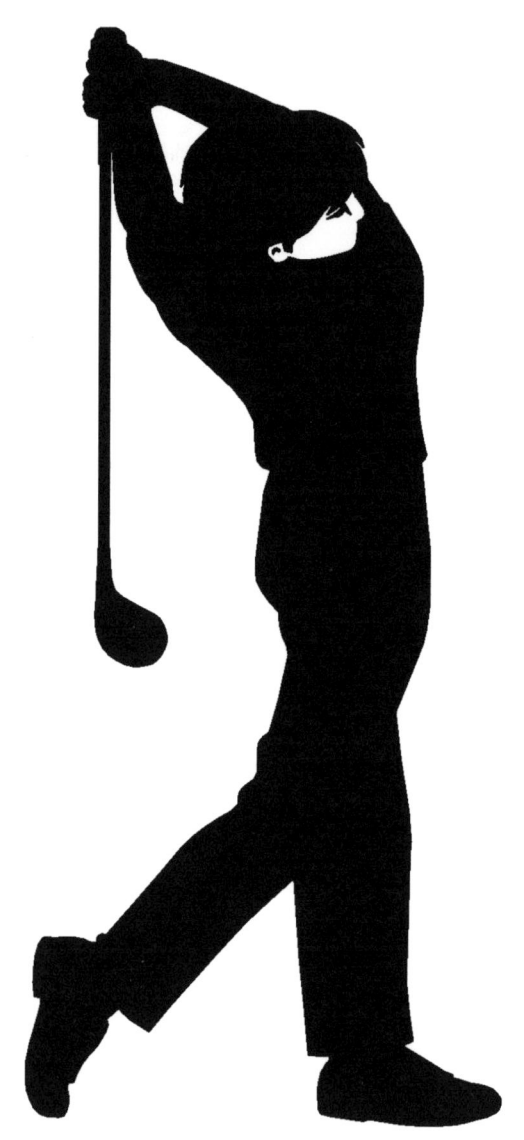

NUMBER 24

PLAY TO YOUR HANDICAP

In golf everyone has a handicap unless you are a professional tour player. Ask a golf professional how to establish your handicap. If you can shoot your handicap, you will be a happier golfer and win many golfing bets with your friends. Since most golfers are handicapped in this difficult game, approach each round of golf trying to shoot a score equal to or below your handicap and you will have more fun. If a handicap is legitimate, you will only shoot equal to or below it 25% of the time. Play to your handicap and be realistic about your ability.

NUMBER 23

DO NOT THINK ABOUT YOUR SCORE

When you are hitting good shots and playing smart your score will reflect accordingly. The best scores are those that you are not thinking about and days when you have the fewest number of putts. Worrying about your score will usually lead to a higher score. Don't think about your score.

NUMBER 22

PLAY POSITION GOLF

Always be thinking about the best place to be on your next shot. Example, if the pin is on the right side of the green, play to the left and vice versa. Try to avoid trouble on each hole and your score will improve. Playing position golf will help you lower your scores.

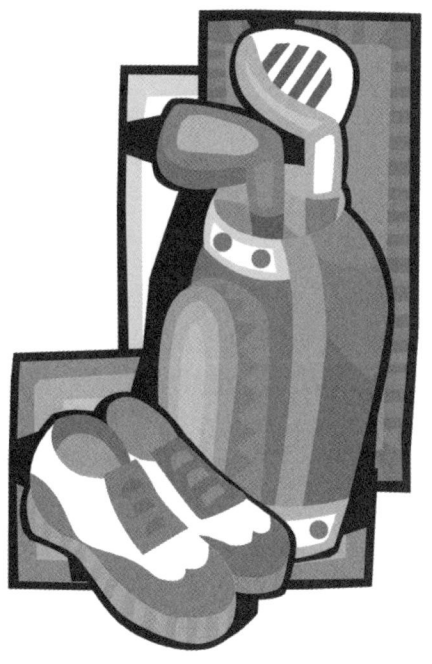

NUMBER 21

BAD HOLES HAPPEN TO EVERYONE

Everyone will have some bad holes during a round of golf. Good players minimize the number of strokes on these bad holes. When you hit a ball out of bounds or in the water, play the hole like the par is 2 strokes higher. Example a par 3 mentally becomes a par 5, a par 4 mentally becomes a par 6, and a par 5 becomes a par 7. This will help you feel more successful on these bad holes that will happen and reduce your overall score.

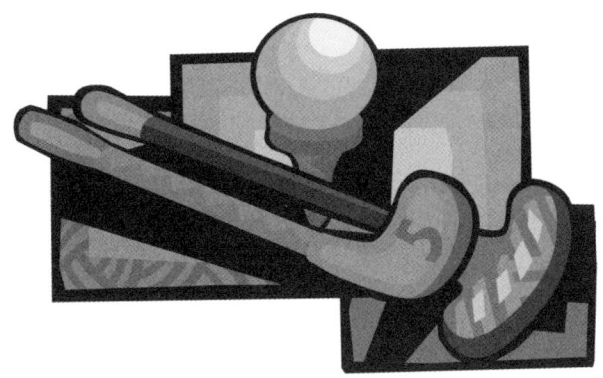

NUMBER 20

COUNTING PENALTY STROKES

It is not fun to recalculate a bad score on a hole. When you incurred penalty strokes, it can be even more miserable determining your score. The easy way to add your score on a bad hole is to determine how many times you hit the ball then add the proper penalty 1 or 2 strokes. Carry a rulebook to determine the proper penalty. More importantly, forget about that hole as quickly as possible and move on to the next hole with a clear mind.

NUMBER 19

WHAT WATER

Good golfers do not see water before they hit their shots over lakes or streams. If you think you cannot get over the water, you probably won't make it. Save yourself some strokes by hitting short of the water and then hitting your next shot over it.

NUMBER 18

BAD LUCK WILL HAPPEN

Don't get discouraged when you get a bad bounce during the game of golf. Erase these incidents out of your mind and concentrate on your next shot. Bad luck will happen.

NUMBER 17

EXPECT GOOD LUCK

In this game you will get good and bad bounces just like life. When you expect good luck, it will happen. Always expect good luck.

NUMBER 16

LEARN TO HIT A LOB SHOT 60 DEGREE WEDGE

This shot will help you get closer to the hole and reduce your score on difficult chip shots. Ask your local professional to show you how to hit this shot.

NUMBER 15

LEARN TO LOVE THE SAND

Sand shots are very easy unless your ball is buried in the sand, under the lip of a sand trap, or in one of the famous St. Andrews, Scotland pot bunkers. Learn to love this shot, as it will improve your score. Simply, hit two inches behind the ball and follow thru with your shot. You will love the results. Practice this shot at the range and learn to love the sand.

NUMBER 14

EXPECT AN ACE ON EVERY PAR THREE

Even if you do not get a hole in one, this thinking will get you closer to the hole a large percentage of the time and hopefully experience the pinnacle of golf, a hole in one. Aces happen every day, however your odds of getting one are 1-20,000 to 1-33,000 per the US Golf register.

NUMBER 13

CARRY A WARM-UP CLUB

A weighted club with a molded grip will help you warm up before teeing off especially if you do not have time to hit balls at the range. The grip is a very important part of the golf swing. A molded grip on your weighted practice club will help you attain proper muscle memory and help you shoot lower scores. The club can be carried in your bag but cannot be used without incurring a penalty once your round has started. Keep the club in your office or home and swing it each day. You can purchase one at most golf shops.

NUMBER 12

USE THE PROPER TEES

The best golfers should use the back tees. The game is hard enough from the proper tees. If you are not sure what tees to use, ask the pro before teeing off. You will enjoy your round much more, be properly challenged and speed up play with a goal of finishing 18 holes in 4 hours or less. Use the proper tees based on your skill level.

NUMBER 11

PLAY GOOD, PLAY BAD, PLAY FAST

Do not waste too much time thinking about your golf shots or putts. Make a decision on the club to be used and do not second-guess yourself. Everyone should try and play 18 holes of golf in 4 hours or less. Play good, play bad, play fast.

NUMBER 10

TURN OFF YOUR CELL PHONE

Focus on playing golf. If you are thinking about other issues, your scores will rise. Turn off your cell phone and come to the golf course with a clear mind. You will shoot lower scores and have more fun.

NUMBER 9

GET YOUR EQUIPMENT PROPERLY FITTED

Buy equipment that is properly fitted to your swing speed, and physical make-up. Proper shafts, lofts, grip size etc. will help you improve your score. Get advice from a club fitter or professional not from a friend who shoots high scores.

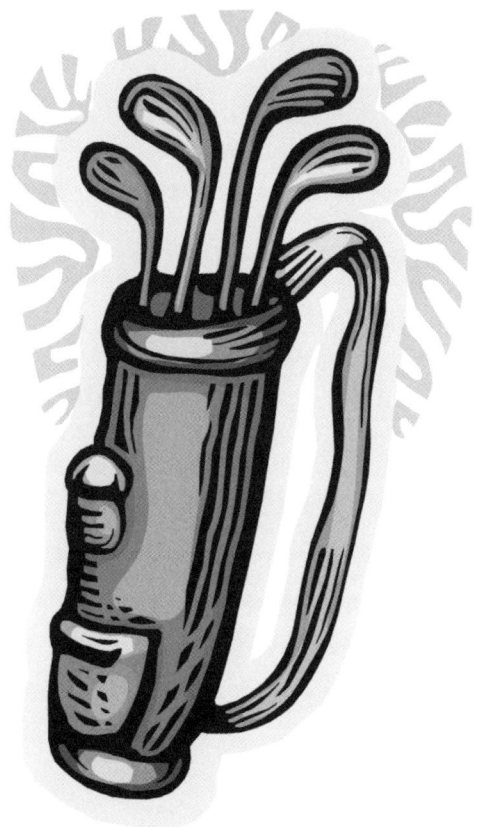

NUMBER 8

TRY AND MAKE EVERY CHIP SHOT

When chipping the ball (short shots near the green), try and make the shot rather than just get on the green. Increasing your expectation level will result in more chip shots going into the hole. In addition, more shots will get closer to the hole rather than just getting on the green. Take a lesson from your golf professional on the various types of short shots that you can use. Practice these shots; they will lower your score.

NUMBER 7

TAKE YOUR MEDICINE

When you have a bad hole and you will, minimize your number of strokes by hitting the ball back into the fairway. Trying difficult shots might be fun but takes lots of skill and will increase your score most of the time. Take your medicine and get the ball back into play and you will reduce your score.

NUMBER 6

ACCURACY IS MORE IMPORTANT THAN DISTANCE

Practice aiming at a target off the tee and hitting an accurate drive into the fairway. Most golfers naturally hit the ball either left to right or right to left. Don't fight this natural tendency. Instead play the ball that you naturally hit (if you hit it right, aim a little left and vice versa). Greens keepers spend a lot of time on grooming the fairways to perfection. Hitting the ball into the fairway makes the hole much easier and will lower your score. Accuracy is more important than distance.

NUMBER 5

WHEN YOU REALLY UNDERSTAND THE GAME OF GOLF, IT IS ALL ABOUT BEING A GOOD PUTTER

A good putt makes a bad hole good and a good hole great. Good putters expect to make every putt. They also have great distance control. When they miss a putt, it is usually very close to the hole. In addition, good putters have a consistent pre-putt routine. Example: they line up the ball, swing the putter twice, and then putt the ball. Develop a pre-shot routine that is comfortable and quick for you. Putting represents 50% or more shots in golf. Practice your putting and your score will improve. Golf is all about being a good putter.

NUMBER 4

A GREAT SHORT GAME WILL LOWER YOUR SCORE

Practice your short game. Practicing shots 100 yards or less will lower your scores. 75% of the shots in golf are 100 yards or less. A short game lesson from your professional will improve your game and lower your score.

NUMBER 3

DO NOT GET MENTALLY CONFUSED

Golf lessons focus too much on the mechanics of golf and not enough on the mental aspects of the game. Trying to remember more than 1 thought during a golf swing will probably result in a bad shot. Focus on 1 thing, hitting a solid golf shot. If you take lessons, get them from a golf professional not from a friend who shoots high scores. Don't get mentally confused and you will lower your score.

NUMBER 2

MOST SHOTS ARE PERFECT

Some shots are more perfect than others. However, don't be so hard on yourself. If the ball is in play, it is perfect. Concentrate on making solid contact every time you hit the ball. Anything can and will happen in golf. Never give up. Your next shot could go into the hole. Most shots are perfect.

NUMBER 1

**THE GAME OF GOLF IS 95% MENTAL
AND 5% MENTAL**

Like life, positive golf thoughts lead to positive results, more fun and lowers scores. Tell yourself you are the best golfer in the world before each drive, pitch, or putt. You will be pleased with the results. Enjoy this great game Practice, Practice, Practice and remember Golf is 95% mental and 5% mental.